C-2606 CAREER EXAMINATION SERIES

This is your
PASSBOOK for...

Administrative Park & Recreation Manager

Test Preparation Study Guide
Questions & Answers

COPYRIGHT NOTICE

This book is SOLELY intended for, is sold ONLY to, and its use is RESTRICTED to individual, bona fide applicants or candidates who qualify by virtue of having seriously filed applications for appropriate license, certificate, professional and/or promotional advancement, higher school matriculation, scholarship, or other legitimate requirements of education and/or governmental authorities.

This book is NOT intended for use, class instruction, tutoring, training, duplication, copying, reprinting, excerption, or adaptation, etc., by:

1) Other publishers
2) Proprietors and/or Instructors of "Coaching" and/or Preparatory Courses
3) Personnel and/or Training Divisions of commercial, industrial, and governmental organizations
4) Schools, colleges, or universities and/or their departments and staffs, including teachers and other personnel
5) Testing Agencies or Bureaus
6) Study groups which seek by the purchase of a single volume to copy and/or duplicate and/or adapt this material for use by the group as a whole without having purchased individual volumes for each of the members of the group
7) Et al.

Such persons would be in violation of appropriate Federal and State statutes.

PROVISION OF LICENSING AGREEMENTS – Recognized educational, commercial, industrial, and governmental institutions and organizations, and others legitimately engaged in educational pursuits, including training, testing, and measurement activities, may address request for a licensing agreement to the copyright owners, who will determine whether, and under what conditions, including fees and charges, the materials in this book may be used them. In other words, a licensing facility exists for the legitimate use of the material in this book on other than an individual basis. However, it is asseverated and affirmed here that the material in this book CANNOT be used without the receipt of the express permission of such a licensing agreement from the Publishers. Inquiries re licensing should be addressed to the company, attention rights and permissions department.

All rights reserved, including the right of reproduction in whole or in part, in any form or by any means, electronic or mechanical, including photocopying, recording, or by any information storage and retrieval system, without permission in writing from the Publisher.

Copyright © 2024 by
National Learning Corporation

212 Michael Drive, Syosset, NY 11791
(516) 921-8888 • www.passbooks.com
E-mail: info@passbooks.com

PUBLISHED IN THE UNITED STATES OF AMERICA

PASSBOOK® SERIES

THE *PASSBOOK® SERIES* has been created to prepare applicants and candidates for the ultimate academic battlefield – the examination room.

At some time in our lives, each and every one of us may be required to take an examination – for validation, matriculation, admission, qualification, registration, certification, or licensure.

Based on the assumption that every applicant or candidate has met the basic formal educational standards, has taken the required number of courses, and read the necessary texts, the *PASSBOOK® SERIES* furnishes the one special preparation which may assure passing with confidence, instead of failing with insecurity. Examination questions – together with answers – are furnished as the basic vehicle for study so that the mysteries of the examination and its compounding difficulties may be eliminated or diminished by a sure method.

This book is meant to help you pass your examination provided that you qualify and are serious in your objective.

The entire field is reviewed through the huge store of content information which is succinctly presented through a provocative and challenging approach – the question-and-answer method.

A climate of success is established by furnishing the correct answers at the end of each test.

You soon learn to recognize types of questions, forms of questions, and patterns of questioning. You may even begin to anticipate expected outcomes.

You perceive that many questions are repeated or adapted so that you can gain acute insights, which may enable you to score many sure points.

You learn how to confront new questions, or types of questions, and to attack them confidently and work out the correct answers.

You note objectives and emphases, and recognize pitfalls and dangers, so that you may make positive educational adjustments.

Moreover, you are kept fully informed in relation to new concepts, methods, practices, and directions in the field.

You discover that you are actually taking the examination all the time: you are preparing for the examination by "taking" an examination, not by reading extraneous and/or supererogatory textbooks.

In short, this PASSBOOK®, used directedly, should be an important factor in helping you to pass your test.

ADMINISTRATIVE PARK AND RECREATION MANAGER

DUTIES AND RESPONSIBILITIES
This is a management class of positions with several assignment levels. Under executive or general direction, with varying degrees of latitude for the exercise of independent judgment, is responsible for maintenance and operations and/or recreation programs, projects, and activities for various Department of Parks and Recreation facilities; performs related work.

SCOPE OF THE EXAMINATION
The written test may include questions on planning and managing the maintenance and operations of park facilities and/or recreational programs; recruiting, training, and supervising staff; conducting meetings; dealing with public and community groups; and standards of employee conduct; and other related areas.

HOW TO TAKE A TEST

I. YOU MUST PASS AN EXAMINATION

A. WHAT EVERY CANDIDATE SHOULD KNOW

Examination applicants often ask us for help in preparing for the written test. What can I study in advance? What kinds of questions will be asked? How will the test be given? How will the papers be graded?

As an applicant for a civil service examination, you may be wondering about some of these things. Our purpose here is to suggest effective methods of advance study and to describe civil service examinations.

Your chances for success on this examination can be increased if you know how to prepare. Those "pre-examination jitters" can be reduced if you know what to expect. You can even experience an adventure in good citizenship if you know why civil service exams are given.

B. WHY ARE CIVIL SERVICE EXAMINATIONS GIVEN?

Civil service examinations are important to you in two ways. As a citizen, you want public jobs filled by employees who know how to do their work. As a job seeker, you want a fair chance to compete for that job on an equal footing with other candidates. The best-known means of accomplishing this two-fold goal is the competitive examination.

Exams are widely publicized throughout the nation. They may be administered for jobs in federal, state, city, municipal, town or village governments or agencies.

Any citizen may apply, with some limitations, such as the age or residence of applicants. Your experience and education may be reviewed to see whether you meet the requirements for the particular examination. When these requirements exist, they are reasonable and applied consistently to all applicants. Thus, a competitive examination may cause you some uneasiness now, but it is your privilege and safeguard.

C. HOW ARE CIVIL SERVICE EXAMS DEVELOPED?

Examinations are carefully written by trained technicians who are specialists in the field known as "psychological measurement," in consultation with recognized authorities in the field of work that the test will cover. These experts recommend the subject matter areas or skills to be tested; only those knowledges or skills important to your success on the job are included. The most reliable books and source materials available are used as references. Together, the experts and technicians judge the difficulty level of the questions.

Test technicians know how to phrase questions so that the problem is clearly stated. Their ethics do not permit "trick" or "catch" questions. Questions may have been tried out on sample groups, or subjected to statistical analysis, to determine their usefulness.

Written tests are often used in combination with performance tests, ratings of training and experience, and oral interviews. All of these measures combine to form the best-known means of finding the right person for the right job.

II. HOW TO PASS THE WRITTEN TEST

A. NATURE OF THE EXAMINATION

To prepare intelligently for civil service examinations, you should know how they differ from school examinations you have taken. In school you were assigned certain definite pages to read or subjects to cover. The examination questions were quite detailed and usually emphasized memory. Civil service exams, on the other hand, try to discover your present ability to perform the duties of a position, plus your potentiality to learn these duties. In other words, a civil service exam attempts to predict how successful you will be. Questions cover such a broad area that they cannot be as minute and detailed as school exam questions.

In the public service similar kinds of work, or positions, are grouped together in one "class." This process is known as *position-classification*. All the positions in a class are paid according to the salary range for that class. One class title covers all of these positions, and they are all tested by the same examination.

B. FOUR BASIC STEPS

1) Study the announcement

How, then, can you know what subjects to study? Our best answer is: "Learn as much as possible about the class of positions for which you've applied." The exam will test the knowledge, skills and abilities needed to do the work.

Your most valuable source of information about the position you want is the official exam announcement. This announcement lists the training and experience qualifications. Check these standards and apply only if you come reasonably close to meeting them.

The brief description of the position in the examination announcement offers some clues to the subjects which will be tested. Think about the job itself. Review the duties in your mind. Can you perform them, or are there some in which you are rusty? Fill in the blank spots in your preparation.

Many jurisdictions preview the written test in the exam announcement by including a section called "Knowledge and Abilities Required," "Scope of the Examination," or some similar heading. Here you will find out specifically what fields will be tested.

2) Review your own background

Once you learn in general what the position is all about, and what you need to know to do the work, ask yourself which subjects you already know fairly well and which need improvement. You may wonder whether to concentrate on improving your strong areas or on building some background in your fields of weakness. When the announcement has specified "some knowledge" or "considerable knowledge," or has used adjectives like "beginning principles of…" or "advanced … methods," you can get a clue as to the number and difficulty of questions to be asked in any given field. More questions, and hence broader coverage, would be included for those subjects which are more important in the work. Now weigh your strengths and weaknesses against the job requirements and prepare accordingly.

3) Determine the level of the position

Another way to tell how intensively you should prepare is to understand the level of the job for which you are applying. Is it the entering level? In other words, is this the position in which beginners in a field of work are hired? Or is it an intermediate or advanced level? Sometimes this is indicated by such words as "Junior" or "Senior" in the class title. Other jurisdictions use Roman numerals to designate the level – Clerk I, Clerk II, for example. The word "Supervisor" sometimes appears in the title. If the level is not indicated by the title, check the description of duties. Will you be working under very close supervision, or will you have responsibility for independent decisions in this work?

4) Choose appropriate study materials

Now that you know the subjects to be examined and the relative amount of each subject to be covered, you can choose suitable study materials. For beginning level jobs, or even advanced ones, if you have a pronounced weakness in some aspect of your training, read a modern, standard textbook in that field. Be sure it is up to date and has general coverage. Such books are normally available at your library, and the librarian will be glad to help you locate one. For entry-level positions, questions of appropriate difficulty are chosen – neither highly advanced questions, nor those too simple. Such questions require careful thought but not advanced training.

If the position for which you are applying is technical or advanced, you will read more advanced, specialized material. If you are already familiar with the basic principles of your field, elementary textbooks would waste your time. Concentrate on advanced textbooks and technical periodicals. Think through the concepts and review difficult problems in your field.

These are all general sources. You can get more ideas on your own initiative, following these leads. For example, training manuals and publications of the government agency which employs workers in your field can be useful, particularly for technical and professional positions. A letter or visit to the government department involved may result in more specific study suggestions, and certainly will provide you with a more definite idea of the exact nature of the position you are seeking.

III. KINDS OF TESTS

Tests are used for purposes other than measuring knowledge and ability to perform specified duties. For some positions, it is equally important to test ability to make adjustments to new situations or to profit from training. In others, basic mental abilities not dependent on information are essential. Questions which test these things may not appear as pertinent to the duties of the position as those which test for knowledge and information. Yet they are often highly important parts of a fair examination. For very general questions, it is almost impossible to help you direct your study efforts. What we can do is to point out some of the more common of these general abilities needed in public service positions and describe some typical questions.

1) General information

Broad, general information has been found useful for predicting job success in some kinds of work. This is tested in a variety of ways, from vocabulary lists to questions about current events. Basic background in some field of work, such as sociology or economics, may be sampled in a group of questions. Often these are principles which have become familiar to most persons through exposure rather than through formal training. It is difficult to advise you how to study for these questions; being alert to the world around you is our best suggestion.

2) Verbal ability

An example of an ability needed in many positions is verbal or language ability. Verbal ability is, in brief, the ability to use and understand words. Vocabulary and grammar tests are typical measures of this ability. Reading comprehension or paragraph interpretation questions are common in many kinds of civil service tests. You are given a paragraph of written material and asked to find its central meaning.

3) Numerical ability

Number skills can be tested by the familiar arithmetic problem, by checking paired lists of numbers to see which are alike and which are different, or by interpreting charts and graphs. In the latter test, a graph may be printed in the test booklet which you are asked to use as the basis for answering questions.

4) Observation

A popular test for law-enforcement positions is the observation test. A picture is shown to you for several minutes, then taken away. Questions about the picture test your ability to observe both details and larger elements.

5) Following directions

In many positions in the public service, the employee must be able to carry out written instructions dependably and accurately. You may be given a chart with several columns, each column listing a variety of information. The questions require you to carry out directions involving the information given in the chart.

6) Skills and aptitudes

Performance tests effectively measure some manual skills and aptitudes. When the skill is one in which you are trained, such as typing or shorthand, you can practice. These tests are often very much like those given in business school or high school courses. For many of the other skills and aptitudes, however, no short-time preparation can be made. Skills and abilities natural to you or that you have developed throughout your lifetime are being tested.

Many of the general questions just described provide all the data needed to answer the questions and ask you to use your reasoning ability to find the answers. Your best preparation for these tests, as well as for tests of facts and ideas, is to be at your physical and mental best. You, no doubt, have your own methods of getting into an exam-taking mood and keeping "in shape." The next section lists some ideas on this subject.

IV. KINDS OF QUESTIONS

Only rarely is the "essay" question, which you answer in narrative form, used in civil service tests. Civil service tests are usually of the short-answer type. Full instructions for answering these questions will be given to you at the examination. But in case this is your first experience with short-answer questions and separate answer sheets, here is what you need to know:

1) Multiple-choice Questions

Most popular of the short-answer questions is the "multiple choice" or "best answer" question. It can be used, for example, to test for factual knowledge, ability to solve problems or judgment in meeting situations found at work.

A multiple-choice question is normally one of three types—

- It can begin with an incomplete statement followed by several possible endings. You are to find the one ending which *best* completes the statement, although some of the others may not be entirely wrong.
- It can also be a complete statement in the form of a question which is answered by choosing one of the statements listed.

- It can be in the form of a problem – again you select the best answer.

Here is an example of a multiple-choice question with a discussion which should give you some clues as to the method for choosing the right answer:

When an employee has a complaint about his assignment, the action which will *best* help him overcome his difficulty is to
    A. discuss his difficulty with his coworkers
    B. take the problem to the head of the organization
    C. take the problem to the person who gave him the assignment
    D. say nothing to anyone about his complaint

In answering this question, you should study each of the choices to find which is best. Consider choice "A" – Certainly an employee may discuss his complaint with fellow employees, but no change or improvement can result, and the complaint remains unresolved. Choice "B" is a poor choice since the head of the organization probably does not know what assignment you have been given, and taking your problem to him is known as "going over the head" of the supervisor. The supervisor, or person who made the assignment, is the person who can clarify it or correct any injustice. Choice "C" is, therefore, correct. To say nothing, as in choice "D," is unwise. Supervisors have and interest in knowing the problems employees are facing, and the employee is seeking a solution to his problem.

2) True/False Questions

The "true/false" or "right/wrong" form of question is sometimes used. Here a complete statement is given. Your job is to decide whether the statement is right or wrong.

SAMPLE: A roaming cell-phone call to a nearby city costs less than a non-roaming call to a distant city.

This statement is wrong, or false, since roaming calls are more expensive.

This is not a complete list of all possible question forms, although most of the others are variations of these common types. You will always get complete directions for answering questions. Be sure you understand *how* to mark your answers – ask questions until you do.

V. RECORDING YOUR ANSWERS

Computer terminals are used more and more today for many different kinds of exams.
For an examination with very few applicants, you may be told to record your answers in the test booklet itself. Separate answer sheets are much more common. If this separate answer sheet is to be scored by machine – and this is often the case – it is highly important that you mark your answers correctly in order to get credit.
An electronic scoring machine is often used in civil service offices because of the speed with which papers can be scored. Machine-scored answer sheets must be marked with a pencil, which will be given to you. This pencil has a high graphite content which responds to the electronic scoring machine. As a matter of fact, stray dots may register as answers, so do not let your pencil rest on the answer sheet while you are pondering the correct answer. Also, if your pencil lead breaks or is otherwise defective, ask for another.

Since the answer sheet will be dropped in a slot in the scoring machine, be careful not to bend the corners or get the paper crumpled.

The answer sheet normally has five vertical columns of numbers, with 30 numbers to a column. These numbers correspond to the question numbers in your test booklet. After each number, going across the page are four or five pairs of dotted lines. These short dotted lines have small letters or numbers above them. The first two pairs may also have a "T" or "F" above the letters. This indicates that the first two pairs only are to be used if the questions are of the true-false type. If the questions are multiple choice, disregard the "T" and "F" and pay attention only to the small letters or numbers.

Answer your questions in the manner of the sample that follows:

32. The largest city in the United States is
    A. Washington, D.C.
    B. New York City
    C. Chicago
    D. Detroit
    E. San Francisco

1) Choose the answer you think is best. (New York City is the largest, so "B" is correct.)
2) Find the row of dotted lines numbered the same as the question you are answering. (Find row number 32)
3) Find the pair of dotted lines corresponding to the answer. (Find the pair of lines under the mark "B.")
4) Make a solid black mark between the dotted lines.

VI. BEFORE THE TEST

Common sense will help you find procedures to follow to get ready for an examination. Too many of us, however, overlook these sensible measures. Indeed, nervousness and fatigue have been found to be the most serious reasons why applicants fail to do their best on civil service tests. Here is a list of reminders:

- Begin your preparation early – Don't wait until the last minute to go scurrying around for books and materials or to find out what the position is all about.
- Prepare continuously – An hour a night for a week is better than an all-night cram session. This has been definitely established. What is more, a night a week for a month will return better dividends than crowding your study into a shorter period of time.
- Locate the place of the exam – You have been sent a notice telling you when and where to report for the examination. If the location is in a different town or otherwise unfamiliar to you, it would be well to inquire the best route and learn something about the building.
- Relax the night before the test – Allow your mind to rest. Do not study at all that night. Plan some mild recreation or diversion; then go to bed early and get a good night's sleep.
- Get up early enough to make a leisurely trip to the place for the test – This way unforeseen events, traffic snarls, unfamiliar buildings, etc. will not upset you.
- Dress comfortably – A written test is not a fashion show. You will be known by number and not by name, so wear something comfortable.

- Leave excess paraphernalia at home – Shopping bags and odd bundles will get in your way. You need bring only the items mentioned in the official notice you received; usually everything you need is provided. Do not bring reference books to the exam. They will only confuse those last minutes and be taken away from you when in the test room.
- Arrive somewhat ahead of time – If because of transportation schedules you must get there very early, bring a newspaper or magazine to take your mind off yourself while waiting.
- Locate the examination room – When you have found the proper room, you will be directed to the seat or part of the room where you will sit. Sometimes you are given a sheet of instructions to read while you are waiting. Do not fill out any forms until you are told to do so; just read them and be prepared.
- Relax and prepare to listen to the instructions
- If you have any physical problem that may keep you from doing your best, be sure to tell the test administrator. If you are sick or in poor health, you really cannot do your best on the exam. You can come back and take the test some other time.

VII. AT THE TEST

The day of the test is here and you have the test booklet in your hand. The temptation to get going is very strong. Caution! There is more to success than knowing the right answers. You must know how to identify your papers and understand variations in the type of short-answer question used in this particular examination. Follow these suggestions for maximum results from your efforts:

1) Cooperate with the monitor

The test administrator has a duty to create a situation in which you can be as much at ease as possible. He will give instructions, tell you when to begin, check to see that you are marking your answer sheet correctly, and so on. He is not there to guard you, although he will see that your competitors do not take unfair advantage. He wants to help you do your best.

2) Listen to all instructions

Don't jump the gun! Wait until you understand all directions. In most civil service tests you get more time than you need to answer the questions. So don't be in a hurry. Read each word of instructions until you clearly understand the meaning. Study the examples, listen to all announcements and follow directions. Ask questions if you do not understand what to do.

3) Identify your papers

Civil service exams are usually identified by number only. You will be assigned a number; you must not put your name on your test papers. Be sure to copy your number correctly. Since more than one exam may be given, copy your exact examination title.

4) Plan your time

Unless you are told that a test is a "speed" or "rate of work" test, speed itself is usually not important. Time enough to answer all the questions will be provided, but this does not mean that you have all day. An overall time limit has been set. Divide the total time (in minutes) by the number of questions to determine the approximate time you have for each question.

5) Do not linger over difficult questions

If you come across a difficult question, mark it with a paper clip (useful to have along) and come back to it when you have been through the booklet. One caution if you do this – be sure to skip a number on your answer sheet as well. Check often to be sure that you have not lost your place and that you are marking in the row numbered the same as the question you are answering.

6) Read the questions

Be sure you know what the question asks! Many capable people are unsuccessful because they failed to *read* the questions correctly.

7) Answer all questions

Unless you have been instructed that a penalty will be deducted for incorrect answers, it is better to guess than to omit a question.

8) Speed tests

It is often better NOT to guess on speed tests. It has been found that on timed tests people are tempted to spend the last few seconds before time is called in marking answers at random – without even reading them – in the hope of picking up a few extra points. To discourage this practice, the instructions may warn you that your score will be "corrected" for guessing. That is, a penalty will be applied. The incorrect answers will be deducted from the correct ones, or some other penalty formula will be used.

9) Review your answers

If you finish before time is called, go back to the questions you guessed or omitted to give them further thought. Review other answers if you have time.

10) Return your test materials

If you are ready to leave before others have finished or time is called, take ALL your materials to the monitor and leave quietly. Never take any test material with you. The monitor can discover whose papers are not complete, and taking a test booklet may be grounds for disqualification.

VIII. EXAMINATION TECHNIQUES

1) Read the general instructions carefully. These are usually printed on the first page of the exam booklet. As a rule, these instructions refer to the timing of the examination; the fact that you should not start work until the signal and must stop work at a signal, etc. If there are any *special* instructions, such as a choice of questions to be answered, make sure that you note this instruction carefully.

2) When you are ready to start work on the examination, that is as soon as the signal has been given, read the instructions to each question booklet, underline any key words or phrases, such as *least, best, outline, describe* and the like. In this way you will tend to answer as requested rather than discover on reviewing your paper that you *listed without describing*, that you selected the *worst* choice rather than the *best* choice, etc.

3) If the examination is of the objective or multiple-choice type – that is, each question will also give a series of possible answers: A, B, C or D, and you are called upon to select the best answer and write the letter next to that answer on your answer paper – it is advisable to start answering each question in turn. There may be anywhere from 50 to 100 such questions in the three or four hours allotted and you can see how much time would be taken if you read through all the questions before beginning to answer any. Furthermore, if you come across a question or group of questions which you know would be difficult to answer, it would undoubtedly affect your handling of all the other questions.

4) If the examination is of the essay type and contains but a few questions, it is a moot point as to whether you should read all the questions before starting to answer any one. Of course, if you are given a choice – say five out of seven and the like – then it is essential to read all the questions so you can eliminate the two that are most difficult. If, however, you are asked to answer all the questions, there may be danger in trying to answer the easiest one first because you may find that you will spend too much time on it. The best technique is to answer the first question, then proceed to the second, etc.

5) Time your answers. Before the exam begins, write down the time it started, then add the time allowed for the examination and write down the time it must be completed, then divide the time available somewhat as follows:
    - If 3-1/2 hours are allowed, that would be 210 minutes. If you have 80 objective-type questions, that would be an average of 2-1/2 minutes per question. Allow yourself no more than 2 minutes per question, or a total of 160 minutes, which will permit about 50 minutes to review.
    - If for the time allotment of 210 minutes there are 7 essay questions to answer, that would average about 30 minutes a question. Give yourself only 25 minutes per question so that you have about 35 minutes to review.

6) The most important instruction is to *read each question* and make sure you know what is wanted. The second most important instruction is to *time yourself properly* so that you answer every question. The third most important instruction is to *answer every question*. Guess if you have to but include something for each question. Remember that you will receive no credit for a blank and will probably receive some credit if you write something in answer to an essay question. If you guess a letter – say "B" for a multiple-choice question – you may have guessed right. If you leave a blank as an answer to a multiple-choice question, the examiners may respect your feelings but it will not add a point to your score. Some exams may penalize you for wrong answers, so in such cases *only*, you may not want to guess unless you have some basis for your answer.

7) Suggestions
    a. Objective-type questions
        1. Examine the question booklet for proper sequence of pages and questions
        2. Read all instructions carefully
        3. Skip any question which seems too difficult; return to it after all other questions have been answered
        4. Apportion your time properly; do not spend too much time on any single question or group of questions

5. Note and underline key words – *all, most, fewest, least, best, worst, same, opposite*, etc.
6. Pay particular attention to negatives
7. Note unusual option, e.g., unduly long, short, complex, different or similar in content to the body of the question
8. Observe the use of "hedging" words – *probably, may, most likely*, etc.
9. Make sure that your answer is put next to the same number as the question
10. Do not second-guess unless you have good reason to believe the second answer is definitely more correct
11. Cross out original answer if you decide another answer is more accurate; do not erase until you are ready to hand your paper in
12. Answer all questions; guess unless instructed otherwise
13. Leave time for review

  b. Essay questions
1. Read each question carefully
2. Determine exactly what is wanted. Underline key words or phrases.
3. Decide on outline or paragraph answer
4. Include many different points and elements unless asked to develop any one or two points or elements
5. Show impartiality by giving pros and cons unless directed to select one side only
6. Make and write down any assumptions you find necessary to answer the questions
7. Watch your English, grammar, punctuation and choice of words
8. Time your answers; don't crowd material

8) Answering the essay question

Most essay questions can be answered by framing the specific response around several key words or ideas. Here are a few such key words or ideas:

M's: manpower, materials, methods, money, management
P's: purpose, program, policy, plan, procedure, practice, problems, pitfalls, personnel, public relations
  a. Six basic steps in handling problems:
1. Preliminary plan and background development
2. Collect information, data and facts
3. Analyze and interpret information, data and facts
4. Analyze and develop solutions as well as make recommendations
5. Prepare report and sell recommendations
6. Install recommendations and follow up effectiveness

  b. Pitfalls to avoid
1. *Taking things for granted* – A statement of the situation does not necessarily imply that each of the elements is necessarily true; for example, a complaint may be invalid and biased so that all that can be taken for granted is that a complaint has been registered

2. *Considering only one side of a situation* – Wherever possible, indicate several alternatives and then point out the reasons you selected the best one
3. *Failing to indicate follow up* – Whenever your answer indicates action on your part, make certain that you will take proper follow-up action to see how successful your recommendations, procedures or actions turn out to be
4. *Taking too long in answering any single question* – Remember to time your answers properly

IX. AFTER THE TEST

Scoring procedures differ in detail among civil service jurisdictions although the general principles are the same. Whether the papers are hand-scored or graded by machine we have described, they are nearly always graded by number. That is, the person who marks the paper knows only the number – never the name – of the applicant. Not until all the papers have been graded will they be matched with names. If other tests, such as training and experience or oral interview ratings have been given, scores will be combined. Different parts of the examination usually have different weights. For example, the written test might count 60 percent of the final grade, and a rating of training and experience 40 percent. In many jurisdictions, veterans will have a certain number of points added to their grades.

After the final grade has been determined, the names are placed in grade order and an eligible list is established. There are various methods for resolving ties between those who get the same final grade – probably the most common is to place first the name of the person whose application was received first. Job offers are made from the eligible list in the order the names appear on it. You will be notified of your grade and your rank as soon as all these computations have been made. This will be done as rapidly as possible.

People who are found to meet the requirements in the announcement are called "eligibles." Their names are put on a list of eligible candidates. An eligible's chances of getting a job depend on how high he stands on this list and how fast agencies are filling jobs from the list.

When a job is to be filled from a list of eligibles, the agency asks for the names of people on the list of eligibles for that job. When the civil service commission receives this request, it sends to the agency the names of the three people highest on this list. Or, if the job to be filled has specialized requirements, the office sends the agency the names of the top three persons who meet these requirements from the general list.

The appointing officer makes a choice from among the three people whose names were sent to him. If the selected person accepts the appointment, the names of the others are put back on the list to be considered for future openings.

That is the rule in hiring from all kinds of eligible lists, whether they are for typist, carpenter, chemist, or something else. For every vacancy, the appointing officer has his choice of any one of the top three eligibles on the list. This explains why the person whose name is on top of the list sometimes does not get an appointment when some of the persons lower on the list do. If the appointing officer chooses the second or third eligible, the No. 1 eligible does not get a job at once, but stays on the list until he is appointed or the list is terminated.

X. HOW TO PASS THE INTERVIEW TEST

The examination for which you applied requires an oral interview test. You have already taken the written test and you are now being called for the interview test – the final part of the formal examination.

You may think that it is not possible to prepare for an interview test and that there are no procedures to follow during an interview. Our purpose is to point out some things you can do in advance that will help you and some good rules to follow and pitfalls to avoid while you are being interviewed.

What is an interview supposed to test?

The written examination is designed to test the technical knowledge and competence of the candidate; the oral is designed to evaluate intangible qualities, not readily measured otherwise, and to establish a list showing the relative fitness of each candidate – as measured against his competitors – for the position sought. Scoring is not on the basis of "right" and "wrong," but on a sliding scale of values ranging from "not passable" to "outstanding." As a matter of fact, it is possible to achieve a relatively low score without a single "incorrect" answer because of evident weakness in the qualities being measured.

Occasionally, an examination may consist entirely of an oral test – either an individual or a group oral. In such cases, information is sought concerning the technical knowledges and abilities of the candidate, since there has been no written examination for this purpose. More commonly, however, an oral test is used to supplement a written examination.

Who conducts interviews?

The composition of oral boards varies among different jurisdictions. In nearly all, a representative of the personnel department serves as chairman. One of the members of the board may be a representative of the department in which the candidate would work. In some cases, "outside experts" are used, and, frequently, a businessman or some other representative of the general public is asked to serve. Labor and management or other special groups may be represented. The aim is to secure the services of experts in the appropriate field.

However the board is composed, it is a good idea (and not at all improper or unethical) to ascertain in advance of the interview who the members are and what groups they represent. When you are introduced to them, you will have some idea of their backgrounds and interests, and at least you will not stutter and stammer over their names.

What should be done before the interview?

While knowledge about the board members is useful and takes some of the surprise element out of the interview, there is other preparation which is more substantive. It *is* possible to prepare for an oral interview – in several ways:

1) Keep a copy of your application and review it carefully before the interview

This may be the only document before the oral board, and the starting point of the interview. Know what education and experience you have listed there, and the sequence and dates of all of it. Sometimes the board will ask you to review the highlights of your experience for them; you should not have to hem and haw doing it.

2) Study the class specification and the examination announcement

Usually, the oral board has one or both of these to guide them. The qualities, characteristics or knowledges required by the position sought are stated in these documents. They offer valuable clues as to the nature of the oral interview. For example, if the job involves supervisory responsibilities, the announcement will usually indicate that knowledge of modern supervisory methods and the qualifications of the candidate as a supervisor will be tested. If so, you can expect such questions, frequently in the form of a hypothetical situation which you are expected to solve. NEVER go into an oral without knowledge of the duties and responsibilities of the job you seek.

3) Think through each qualification required

Try to visualize the kind of questions you would ask if you were a board member. How well could you answer them? Try especially to appraise your own knowledge and background in each area, *measured against the job sought*, and identify any areas in which you are weak. Be critical and realistic – do not flatter yourself.

4) Do some general reading in areas in which you feel you may be weak

For example, if the job involves supervision and your past experience has NOT, some general reading in supervisory methods and practices, particularly in the field of human relations, might be useful. Do NOT study agency procedures or detailed manuals. The oral board will be testing your understanding and capacity, not your memory.

5) Get a good night's sleep and watch your general health and mental attitude

You will want a clear head at the interview. Take care of a cold or any other minor ailment, and of course, no hangovers.

What should be done on the day of the interview?

Now comes the day of the interview itself. Give yourself plenty of time to get there. Plan to arrive somewhat ahead of the scheduled time, particularly if your appointment is in the fore part of the day. If a previous candidate fails to appear, the board might be ready for you a bit early. By early afternoon an oral board is almost invariably behind schedule if there are many candidates, and you may have to wait. Take along a book or magazine to read, or your application to review, but leave any extraneous material in the waiting room when you go in for your interview. In any event, relax and compose yourself.

The matter of dress is important. The board is forming impressions about you – from your experience, your manners, your attitude, and your appearance. Give your personal appearance careful attention. Dress your best, but not your flashiest. Choose conservative, appropriate clothing, and be sure it is immaculate. This is a business interview, and your appearance should indicate that you regard it as such. Besides, being well groomed and properly dressed will help boost your confidence.

Sooner or later, someone will call your name and escort you into the interview room. *This is it.* From here on you are on your own. It is too late for any more preparation. But remember, you asked for this opportunity to prove your fitness, and you are here because your request was granted.

What happens when you go in?

The usual sequence of events will be as follows: The clerk (who is often the board stenographer) will introduce you to the chairman of the oral board, who will introduce you to the other members of the board. Acknowledge the introductions before you sit down. Do not be surprised if you find a microphone facing you or a stenotypist sitting by. Oral interviews are usually recorded in the event of an appeal or other review.

Usually the chairman of the board will open the interview by reviewing the highlights of your education and work experience from your application – primarily for the benefit of the other members of the board, as well as to get the material into the record. Do not interrupt or comment unless there is an error or significant misinterpretation; if that is the case, do not hesitate. But do not quibble about insignificant matters. Also, he will usually ask you some question about your education, experience or your present job – partly to get you to start talking and to establish the interviewing "rapport." He may start the actual questioning, or turn it over to one of the other members. Frequently, each member undertakes the questioning on a particular area, one in which he is perhaps most competent, so you can expect each member to participate in the examination. Because time is limited, you may also expect some rather abrupt switches in the direction the questioning takes, so do not be upset by it. Normally, a board member will not pursue a single line of questioning unless he discovers a particular strength or weakness.

After each member has participated, the chairman will usually ask whether any member has any further questions, then will ask you if you have anything you wish to add. Unless you are expecting this question, it may floor you. Worse, it may start you off on an extended, extemporaneous speech. The board is not usually seeking more information. The question is principally to offer you a last opportunity to present further qualifications or to indicate that you have nothing to add. So, if you feel that a significant qualification or characteristic has been overlooked, it is proper to point it out in a sentence or so. Do not compliment the board on the thoroughness of their examination -- they have been sketchy, and you know it. If you wish, merely say, "No thank you, I have nothing further to add." This is a point where you can "talk yourself out" of a good impression or fail to present an important bit of information. Remember, *you close the interview yourself*.

The chairman will then say, "That is all, Mr. _____, thank you." Do not be startled; the interview is over, and quicker than you think. Thank him, gather your belongings and take your leave. Save your sigh of relief for the other side of the door.

How to put your best foot forward

Throughout this entire process, you may feel that the board individually and collectively is trying to pierce your defenses, seek out your hidden weaknesses and embarrass and confuse you. Actually, this is not true. They are obliged to make an appraisal of your qualifications for the job you are seeking, and they want to see you in your best light. Remember, they must interview all candidates and a non-cooperative candidate may become a failure in spite of their best efforts to bring out his qualifications. Here are 15 suggestions that will help you:

1) Be natural – Keep your attitude confident, not cocky

If you are not confident that you can do the job, do not expect the board to be. Do not apologize for your weaknesses, try to bring out your strong points. The board is interested in a positive, not negative, presentation. Cockiness will antagonize any board member and make him wonder if you are covering up a weakness by a false show of strength.

2) Get comfortable, but don't lounge or sprawl

Sit erectly but not stiffly. A careless posture may lead the board to conclude that you are careless in other things, or at least that you are not impressed by the importance of the occasion. Either conclusion is natural, even if incorrect. Do not fuss with your clothing, a pencil or an ashtray. Your hands may occasionally be useful to emphasize a point; do not let them become a point of distraction.

3) Do not wisecrack or make small talk

This is a serious situation, and your attitude should show that you consider it as such. Further, the time of the board is limited – they do not want to waste it, and neither should you.

4) Do not exaggerate your experience or abilities

In the first place, from information in the application or other interviews and sources, the board may know more about you than you think. Secondly, you probably will not get away with it. An experienced board is rather adept at spotting such a situation, so do not take the chance.

5) If you know a board member, do not make a point of it, yet do not hide it

Certainly you are not fooling him, and probably not the other members of the board. Do not try to take advantage of your acquaintanceship – it will probably do you little good.

6) Do not dominate the interview

Let the board do that. They will give you the clues – do not assume that you have to do all the talking. Realize that the board has a number of questions to ask you, and do not try to take up all the interview time by showing off your extensive knowledge of the answer to the first one.

7) Be attentive

You only have 20 minutes or so, and you should keep your attention at its sharpest throughout. When a member is addressing a problem or question to you, give him your undivided attention. Address your reply principally to him, but do not exclude the other board members.

8) Do not interrupt

A board member may be stating a problem for you to analyze. He will ask you a question when the time comes. Let him state the problem, and wait for the question.

9) Make sure you understand the question

Do not try to answer until you are sure what the question is. If it is not clear, restate it in your own words or ask the board member to clarify it for you. However, do not haggle about minor elements.

10) Reply promptly but not hastily

A common entry on oral board rating sheets is "candidate responded readily," or "candidate hesitated in replies." Respond as promptly and quickly as you can, but do not jump to a hasty, ill-considered answer.

11) Do not be peremptory in your answers

A brief answer is proper – but do not fire your answer back. That is a losing game from your point of view. The board member can probably ask questions much faster than you can answer them.

12) Do not try to create the answer you think the board member wants

He is interested in what kind of mind you have and how it works – not in playing games. Furthermore, he can usually spot this practice and will actually grade you down on it.

13) Do not switch sides in your reply merely to agree with a board member

Frequently, a member will take a contrary position merely to draw you out and to see if you are willing and able to defend your point of view. Do not start a debate, yet do not surrender a good position. If a position is worth taking, it is worth defending.

14) Do not be afraid to admit an error in judgment if you are shown to be wrong

The board knows that you are forced to reply without any opportunity for careful consideration. Your answer may be demonstrably wrong. If so, admit it and get on with the interview.

15) Do not dwell at length on your present job

The opening question may relate to your present assignment. Answer the question but do not go into an extended discussion. You are being examined for a *new* job, not your present one. As a matter of fact, try to phrase ALL your answers in terms of the job for which you are being examined.

Basis of Rating

Probably you will forget most of these "do's" and "don'ts" when you walk into the oral interview room. Even remembering them all will not ensure you a passing grade. Perhaps you did not have the qualifications in the first place. But remembering them will help you to put your best foot forward, without treading on the toes of the board members.

Rumor and popular opinion to the contrary notwithstanding, an oral board wants you to make the best appearance possible. They know you are under pressure – but they also want to see how you respond to it as a guide to what your reaction would be under the pressures of the job you seek. They will be influenced by the degree of poise you display, the personal traits you show and the manner in which you respond.

ABOUT THIS BOOK

This book contains tests divided into Examination Sections. Go through each test, answering every question in the margin. We have also attached a sample answer sheet at the back of the book that can be removed and used. At the end of each test look at the answer key and check your answers. On the ones you got wrong, look at the right answer choice and learn. Do not fill in the answers first. Do not memorize the questions and answers, but understand the answer and principles involved. On your test, the questions will likely be different from the samples. Questions are changed and new ones added. If you understand these past questions you should have success with any changes that arise. Tests may consist of several types of questions. We have additional books on each subject should more study be advisable or necessary for you. Finally, the more you study, the better prepared you will be. This book is intended to be the last thing you study before you walk into the examination room. Prior study of relevant texts is also recommended. NLC publishes some of these in our Fundamental Series. Knowledge and good sense are important factors in passing your exam. Good luck also helps. So now study this Passbook, absorb the material contained within and take that knowledge into the examination. Then do your best to pass that exam.

EXAMINATION SECTION

EXAMINATION SECTION
TEST 1

DIRECTIONS: Each question or incomplete statement is followed by several suggested answers or completions. Select the one that BEST answers the question or completes the statement. *PRINT THE LETTER OF THE CORRECT ANSWER IN THE SPACE AT THE RIGHT.*

1. A *typical* definition of recreation agreed upon by MOST authorities would be
    A. voluntarily chosen leisure activities, for pleasure or personal benefit, meeting community standards and needs
    B. pleasurable activities provided by community agencies without social purpose
    C. whatever people want to do, because they want to do it
    D. purposeful activities, such as anti-delinquency, addiction treatment, or golden age programs, which make use of trips and cultural activities

1.____

2. In the past, it was argued that recreation programs for youth prevented juvenile delinquency.
Today the majority of social work or recreation authorities would MOST probably support the view that
    A. recreation is the key element in any anti-delinquency program
    B. recreation has proved to be of little value in anti-delinquency programs
    C. juvenile delinquents usually are anti-social and disruptive and should be kept out of organized recreation programs
    D. juvenile delinquency treatment requires varied services, including education, job training, recreation, and improved housing

2.____

3. The MAJOR professional organization serving the recreation field in the United States today is the
    A. American Institute of Park and Recreation Practitioners
    B. National Recreation and Park Association
    C. National Recreation Association
    D. American Association for Health, Physical Education, and Recreation

3.____

4. Varied theories of play have been developed by psychologists, philosophers, and others.
One TRADITIONAL theory that sees play as the means through which children prepare for the demands of adult life is the _____ theory.
    A. instinct-practice   B. catharsis
    C. recapitulation   D. relaxation

4.____

5. Which of the following statements BEST supports the self-expression theory of play as developed by Mason and Mitchell?
    A. Activities are engaged in for the purpose of overcoming natural human inertness.

5.____

B. Due to the pressures for self-maintenance and other compulsions, human beings use play as outlets for frustration.
C. Human physiological and anatomical structure are independent of any specific form of play.
D. Because human beings are dynamic animals, activity is a primary need of life.

6. Of the following, the MOST recent psychological theory of play is the 6.____
   A. pleasure principle theory (Freud)
   B. play extraversion theory (Piaget)
   C. arousal or stimulation theory (Berlynne)
   D. aggressive-release theory (Schiller-Spencer-Groos)

7. Generally, the BASIC philosophy of public recreation departments today is to 7.____
   A. serve all groups as fully as possible
   B. place the greatest emphasis on helping the poor
   C. serve primarily the middle and upper classes
   D. concentrate on children and youth

8. The one of the following which is NOT a widely accepted goal of public recreation departments is to 8.____
   A. provide constructive and creative outlets for leisure
   B. meet participants' physical, mental, social, and creative needs
   C. develop large numbers of athletes to play on college or pro teams
   D. strengthen family life and help community unity

9. The growth of the organized recreation movement in the United States was promoted by several social factors. 9.____
   Of the following, the one which did NOT contribute to such growth is
   A. the increase in leisure through the shortened work-week, more holidays, and longer vacations
   B. the development of movies, television, and radio as major forms of entertainment
   C. the general affluence and mobility in society
   D. more liberal attitudes toward leisure on the part of religious, educational, and government authorities

10. Recognition by state certifying boards or departments is one of the formal methods through which professionals in fields such as law or medicine are approved. 10.____
    Today, certification for recreation professionals exists in
    A. a small number of states   B. all fifty states
    C. no states   D. about half the states

11. Supervisors should be able to advise recently appointed recreation workers on the appropriate selection of activities for specific age groups. 11.____
    When planning for after-school recreation activities for boys of elementary-school age, the MOST useful type of game would usually be

A. low-organized games, such as dodge-ball, kick-ball, and relays
B. table games, such as parcheessi, backgammon, and chess
C. encounter games and touching games, like those used in sensitivity groups
D. mental games and contests, such as ghost, coffee-pot, and twenty questions

12. Since anti-social youth are often unwilling to enter highly structured activities and programs, or may be barred from recreation centers, they are frequently not served by community recreation agencies.
Of the following, the BEST way to serve such youth is to
    A. develop entirely new kinds of activities that will appeal to delinquents because of their thrill-seeking nature
    B. organize special community center programs to serve only delinquent youth who have been in trouble with the law
    C. assign roving or street gang workers to make contact with unaffiliated youth and gangs to involve them in constructive activities
    D. wait until they are sent to correctional institutions and then give them concentrated recreation programs there

13. Adolescent girls in youth houses (detention or remand centers) often have poor self-concepts.
Of the following, the TYPICAL approach used by recreation workers in such settings to help these girls improve their self-concepts is to
    A. tell such girls at appropriate times that they are just as good as anybody
    B. organize self-improvement classes to teach skills in make-up, dressing, or modeling
    C. sponsor sports teams, such as basketball or volleyball, which can compete with other institutions
    D. administer personality tests to diagnose their problems

14. Many teenage boys are fascinated by automobiles.
Of the following, a USEFUL way for a creation worker to deal with this interest would be to
    A. sponsor drag-racing meets in a conveniently located park or raceway
    B. develop an automotive hobby car repair club in a community center or nearby garage
    C. arrange a contest to select one boy to go on a trip to the Indianapolis 500 to watch the big race
    D. develop a joint program with a school bus company to train boys as junior bus operators

15. According to the traditional *space standards* employed for the past several decades to measure the need for open space and recreation facilities in American communities, there should be AT LEAST
    A. one neighborhood playground for each 1,500 children under age 12
    B. three acres of outdoor recreation space for each 1,000 residents
    C. one acre of outdoor recreation space for each 100 residents
    D. one community center for each 5,000 children and teenagers

16. *Therapeutic recreation service* is the term applied today to programs which serve the physically, mentally, or socially handicapped.
For BEST results, such programs should be provided in
    A. institutions such as mental hospitals or schools for the mentally handicapped
    B. community settings such as after-care centers or community programs for the physically disabled
    C. both institutional and community settings
    D. private or voluntary facilities

16.____

17. Social group work is BEST defined as a method of social work which
    A. assigns people to groups for intensive psychotherapy as a means of crisis intervention
    B. helps people improve their social functioning and ability to cope with inter-personal problems
    C. utilizes unskilled community people to take over many social work organizations
    D. relies on the leader's ability to mobilize people into effective instruments for community reform

17.____

18. Some recreation departments operate multi-service senior centers which provide social services related to nutrition, health needs, legal, or housing assistance, as well as recreation.
This type of program is regarded by leading authorities in the field of recreation as
    A. usually not the function of a recreation department since it has proved to be a hindrance to customary social and recreational programs
    B. clearly not the function of a recreation department and should be discontinued
    C. an appropriate function of a recreation department and is justified by Federal funding guidelines in this field
    D. an appropriate function of a recreation department only when the program is receiving a grant from the State Department of Aging

18.____

19. The view that MOST social workers generally have of recreation is that it is
    A. almost identical to social work
    B. a competitor with social work for public funds
    C. a medium through which they can involve and work constructively with participants
    D. strictly for fun, without a serious purpose

19.____

20. The three MAJOR areas of social work training and practice are
    A. group work, psychiatric case work, and neighborhood management
    B. community analysis, case work, and agency supervision
    C. group rehabilitation, psychiatric community development, and case work
    D. case work, group work, and community organization

20.____

5 (#1)

21. Which of the following BEST expresses the program objectives of recreation programs provided by the municipal agencies as a whole?
They should
   A. emphasize after-school and summer vacation play programs
   B. provide activities for various age groups
   C. concentrate on programs for younger boys and teenage youth
   D. meet social needs that are unsatisfied by family relationships

21.____

22. Of the following, which is the LEAST appropriate basis for choosing the recreation program activities for a community center, hospital, or other institutions? The
   A. needs and interests of the participants based on their age, sex, socio-economic background, etc.
   B. overall philosophy and goals of the sponsoring agency
   C. ability of the agency to offer certain activities based on its staff resources, facilities, funding, etc.
   D. degree to which prospective participants are personally acquainted with one another

22.____

23. The MOST common approach to developing schedules of program activities in municipal recreation departments is to organize them
   A. on a centralized basis, that is, each central office or county headquarters develops a precise schedule that must be followed in each center or playground
   B. on a *report* system, that is, each center or playground develops its individual schedule and must report daily on which activities were carried out, and which were not
   C. on the basis of seasonal interests, with different schedules being developed for summer, fall, winter, and spring
   D. according to whatever seems to be of interest on a particular day, emphasizing flexibility

23.____

24. A difficult problem in scheduling recreation programs is to have personnel available at needed times.
The BEST approach for dealing with this problem is to
   A. change recreation leadership jobs to the four-day workweek that has become so popular in industry
   B. make leadership assignment schedules more flexible to insure coverage for special events, including evening and weekend activities
   C. assign all personnel a noon-to-8 P.M. daily schedule
   D. convert all full-time leadership jobs into part-time per session positions and then assign these as needed

24.____

25. Ideally, the BEST program schedule for a community recreation center would be one which covers
   A. the full day and evening to permit scheduling for senior citizens, housewives, or pre-schoolers, as well as youth and other adults
   B. from 3:00 P.M. to 10:00 P.M. since this is the time when children and youth are out of school

25.____

5

C. the daily hours of maximum use, based on participant demand, because of the financial limitations of many centers
D. daytime hours only since most people today will not come out at night because of fear of crime

KEY (CORRECT ANSWERS)

1.	A		11.	A
2.	D		12.	C
3.	B		13.	B
4.	A		14.	B
5.	D		15.	C
6.	C		16.	C
7.	A		17.	B
8.	C		18.	C
9.	B		19.	C
10.	A		20.	D

21. B
22. D
23. C
24. B
25. A

TEST 2

DIRECTIONS: Each question or incomplete statement is followed by several suggested answers or completions. Select the one that BEST answers the question or completes the statement. *PRINT THE LETTER OF THE CORRECT ANSWER IN THE SPACE AT THE RIGHT.*

1. Active team games during the summer months of July and August at a neighborhood playground are BEST scheduled for
   A. early afternoon and late evening
   B. Saturday only (morning and afternoon)
   C. morning, late afternoon, and evening
   D. evening only (after 7:30 P.M.

   1.____

2. Various activities help to keep attendance at a summer playground high by building interest and enthusiasm among participants.
   Which of the following is the POOREST example of such activities?
   A. Weekly special events, such as pet shows, bicycle rodeos, hobby fairs, etc.
   B. End-of-summer festivals, carnivals, play-days, exhibitions, etc., for which participants prepare for several weeks
   C. Trips using chartered or public transportation to state parks, swimming pools, etc. for those attending regularly
   D. Daily tutoring programs of remedial education for those who are having difficulty in school

   2.____

3. Of the various types of activities sponsored by public recreation departments, the MOST popular single category, according to national surveys, is
   A. services for the handicapped (such as the mentally handicapped, blind, or physical disabled)
   B. the performing arts (music, drama, and dance)
   C. social activities (clubs, parties, dances, etc.)
   D. sports of all kinds (such as baseball, football, and basketball)

   3.____

4. The MOST typical method of organizing youth sports leagues in public recreation departments is to
   A. encourage recreation leaders to organize and coach several teams themselves, running their own tournaments
   B. reduce competitive play, which is harmful to youth, and concentrate instead on cooperative games
   C. work with community organizations that set up and coach their own teams
   D. have children on each block form their own teams and do their own coaching

   4.____

5. Each craft activity has a specific set of items describing its equipment or process. The following words, *bisque, greenware,* and *slab-construction,* are used in reference to
   A. ceramics   B. metalcrafts
   C. glass-blowing   D. decoupage

   5.____

6. According to their degree of difficulty, various arts and crafts activities are usually suited to different age levels,
   Which of the following would be MOST suited to pre-school children?
   A. Macrame
   B. Watercolor painting
   C. Fingerpainting
   D. Jewelry-making

6.____

7. Among the most popular recreational sport activities are basketball, baseball, and bowling.
   The terms which do NOT apply to any of these three games are
   A. strike, dribble, sacrifice
   B. linebacker, offside, foot-fault
   C. spare, infield, hoop
   D. walking, infield, alley

7.____

8. Which of the following activities would LEAST likely be found in a municipal recreation department's music program?
   A. Rock-and-roll band practice and competition
   B. Chamber music groups
   C. Drum and bugle corps
   D. Informal community singing or folk music activities

8.____

9. Informal dramatics activities are often used with children and teenagers.
   Which of the following would be MOST likely to promote creative dramatic skills and interest among beginners?
   A. One-act play contests with scripts, costumes, and scenery
   B. Choral reading of popular poetry
   C. Memorizing and reciting sections from famous Broadway plays
   D. Improvisational dramatic games, like prop or paper bag plays

9.____

10. In the past, many recreation departments sponsored holiday festivals or special events such as the English May Day Festival.
    Today, the trend is to
    A. have such festivals reflect ethnic group interests such as Black Culture or Hispanic-American Arts
    B. eliminate all such events since there is little interest in them
    C. deal mainly with historical commemorations since these would appeal to traditional patriotism
    D. make festivals *future-minded* by dealing with the Space Age or America of the Future

10.____

11. Of the following types of tournaments, the type which can be completed MOST quickly in individual sports such as fencing or table-tennis is the _____ tournament.
    A. round robin
    B. elimination
    C. challenge (pyramid)
    D. challenge (ladder)

11.____

12. Recreation has been affected by several key trends in psychiatric treatment.
    Which of the following is NOT such a key trend?
    A. Reducing patient populations in large, distant state institutions and setting up local mental health facilities, with after-care or day-clinic programs

12.____

B. Reliance on chemotherapy, which makes patients more receptive to programs
C. The development of activity therapy programs in many hospitals, which include education, recreation, occupational therapy, and similar activities
D. Hiring of psychiatric patients as recreation aides, which may lead to employment after discharge

13. In recreation programs serving the seriously physically handicapped, such as those who have suffered strokes, amputations, etc., the PRIMARY program objective is to
    A. help patients develop potential skills using the facilities of community and out-of-hospital recreational programs
    B. raise funds, through parties, bazaars, special shows, etc., that patients put on to meet special patient needs
    C. use recreation as a specific treatment modality that will restore function, help patients learn to use prosthesis, etc.
    D. make patients accept their limitations and the fact that they cannot participate in many normal recreation activities

14. The majority of mentally handicapped teenagers or young adults live in the community, rather than in institutions. Recreation for such persons has several important goals.
    Of the following, the LEAST appropriate recreation goal for such persons is to
    A. help them improve the poor coordination and overcome the obesity typical of many such persons through physical activity
    B. help them acquire social skills and improve behavior and appearance so they will be able to mingle with others more effectively
    C. provide enjoyable and socially desirable leisure activities in order to make life more satisfying
    D. improve their I.Q.'s in order to help them get better jobs or be able to continue in school

15. Senior centers that serve older persons should meet the important needs of these individuals.
    Of the following, it would be LEAST appropriate for such centers to meet the need for
    A. full-time employment by acting as a placement bureau for center members
    B. modified physical activity to help keep older people active and prevent physical deterioration
    C. social activity to help aging people make friends and avoid isolation
    D. program activities in which older people may do volunteer service in hospitals or in the community

16. In planning a recreation program at a low-income public housing project, it is important to establish an advisory board or council.
Such board or council should represent PRIMARILY the needs and interests of the
    A. civic groups
    B. residents
    C. parent-teacher associations
    D. youth workers

17. Public relations may have many objectives for a public recreation department. Of the following, the LEAST appropriate objective would be to
    A. provide accurate information about the department's overall program to the public at large
    B. encourage attendance and involvement at the department's events and regular programs
    C. build favorable public attitudes and encourage volunteer leadership in the programs
    D. encourage petitions or letter-writing campaigns for increased budgets for the department

18. The one of the following which is the MOST effective method for producing successful public relations is for recreation program administrators to
    A. appear before civil organizations
    B. satisfy users of programs
    C. publish effective brochures, announcements, and reports
    D. employ qualified, indigenous para-professionals

19. If a recreation supervisor were going to publicize a large one-day recreation event in his borough, the BEST way to promote attendance would be to
    A. use newspaper releases and distribute fliers to schools, churches, and temples
    B. place posters advertising the event in store windows
    C. put posters on playground bulletin boards
    D. make a filmstrip about the forthcoming event and distribute prints to civic groups

20. Assume that, as a recreation supervisor, you are directing a community center that has poor participation in programs by local residents.
Of the following, the MOST effective way for you to arouse more public interest would be to
    A. have the publicity office in your department's central office send out newspaper releases about the center
    B. form a neighborhood council to interpret the community's needs to you and help publicize your program
    C. frequent places where local people congregate
    D. plan a panel discussion in a nearby community auditorium to discuss the problem

21. There are several possible approaches to getting community involvement in recreation service.
Of the following, the approach that would usually be LEAST workable would be to
   A. draw up a list of interested parents, clergymen, businessmen, local educators, etc., and invite them to a planning meeting about the neighborhood's recreation program
   B. announce an election to a recreation council, and select a slate of nominees, one for each square block so that local residents can elect their own representatives
   C. inquire as to whether the local Parent-Teachers Association will form a subcommittee interested in youth recreation to assist you
   D. work closely with the local district planning board to insure that they consider recreation as an important community service and to get their advice and help

21.____

22. Whether patients will be able to use their leisure constructively after discharge from the hospital is of vital concern to recreation workers in psychiatric hospitals.
Which of the following approaches would be LEAST useful in assuring continuing recreation service to a patient?
   A. Get a mimeographed list of recreation agencies in a patient's neighborhood and give him this before he is discharged
   B. Visit and talk with staff members of recreation agencies in a patient's neighborhood to make plans for their receiving the discharged patient
   C. Develop joint hospital-community recreation programs in special events, tours, entertainment programs, etc. to build a base of understanding for discharged patients
   D. Help the patient develop skills and interests in activities that will actually be available in his neighborhood after discharge

22.____

23. Therapeutic recreation seeks to help disabled persons enjoy a fuller, happier life. The question of whether they should be segregated in separate programs for the handicapped is an important one.
Which of the following statements about this group is MOST valid?
   A. The non-handicapped in society are usually very sympathetic to the disabled and welcome them in all recreational and social programs.
   B. The handicapped are better off by themselves, in groups with others having similar disabilities, so they will not feel inferior.
   C. It is an important goal to integrate the handicapped with other persons whenever possible, although sometimes it may not be feasible.
   D. The handicapped should, without exception, be mixed with the non-handicapped in recreation programs.

23.____

24. Recreation is usually considered to be a positive force for improving social relations between different racial, ethnic, or socio-economic groups.
Of the following, which is the MOST valid statement about recreation and inter-group relations?

24.____

A. Public recreation is one field in which racial discrimination is not prohibited by law.
B. Recreation workers have an obligation to reflect and agree with the views of those they serve, regardless of the nature of such views.
C. Many of our community recreation programs are heavily racially segregated.
D. Prejudice is an inborn trait which often appears in competitive sports.

25. For minority-group youth, sports often provide upward social mobility into college and subsequent business careers.
However, of the following, a MAJOR problem that arises for such youth in their seeking upward social mobility is that
   A. unscrupulous college sports programs often exploit them
   B. they are unable to satisfactorily relate to members of their peer group
   C. sports fail to provide an outlet for hostility and aggression
   D. religious cults to which they become converted distract them from sports

25.____

KEY (CORRECT ANSWERS)

1.	C	11.	B
2.	D	12.	D
3.	D	13.	A
4.	C	14.	D
5.	A	15.	A
6.	C	16.	B
7.	B	17.	D
8.	B	18.	B
9.	D	19.	A
10.	A	20.	B

21.	B
22.	A
23.	C
24.	C
25.	A

TEST 3

DIRECTIONS: Each question or incomplete statement is followed by several suggested answers or completions. Select the one that BEST answers the question or completes the statement. *PRINT THE LETTER OF THE CORRECT ANSWER IN THE SPACE AT THE RIGHT.*

1. The trend in many recreation and park departments during the past several years has been toward providing special facilities and programs based on user fees and charges.
   The criticism MOST often made against such fees and charges is that
   A. few recreation directors have made serious efforts to serve residents of disadvantaged neighborhoods
   B. it increases the cost of servicing and maintaining facilities and services because standards must be raised
   C. public employees may be tempted to misappropriate funds or may be subject to accusations of dishonesty
   D. poor people may be unable to participate in what should be a publicly-available service

2. With few exceptions, recreation directors have not been able to gain permission to operate programs regularly in school buildings.
   Of the following, the MOST successful way to improve this situation is to
   A. develop relationships and cooperative programs with local school board and district officials, or with individual school principals and custodians
   B. bring a class-action suit against the local schoolboard
   C. collect and submit legally valid petitions to the administration
   D. exert pressure on the schools by denying them use of parks or other recreational facilities for their physical education activities

3. Many hospitals, particularly psychiatric hospitals, have therapists keep regular reports of patient participation in recreation programs.
   Of the following, the BEST use of such reports is to
   A. provide information which may be presented at meetings of the treatment team when the progress of patients is discussed
   B. provide a basis for a daily discussion between the patient and the therapist so the patient knows what is expected of him
   C. justify adverse actions such as denial of recreation privileges or the imposition of personal restrictions
   D. meet the requirements of mental hygiene laws as to standards of treatment and patient progress

4. Much correspondence is likely to come into the central office of a public recreation department.
   Generally, all letters should be answered within one or two days UNLESS
   A. a letter is of a commonplace and unimportant nature
   B. the writer is unreasonably critical of the department
   C. form letters are used in place of personalized correspondence
   D. a letter requires special inquiries or decision-making

5. One major type of report in recreation programs is based on the attendance of participants.
   Such report are GENERALLY considered to be
   A. an excellent quantitative and qualitative basis for evaluating the success of a program
   B. of primary use in operational research involving participant behavior and outcomes
   C. unnecessary since few departments continue to use attendance reports as a basis for funding
   D. quite inaccurate unless attendance counts are done systematically and staff members avoid inflating them

5.____

6. An informal survey of recreation in a hospital showed that patients who engaged regularly in the program were discharged from the hospital earlier than those who did not.
   Based on this information only, it would be MOST valid to say that
   A. such information has validity or meaning only to a qualified medical research person
   B. it is inconclusive whether there exists a cause and effect relationship between participation and discharge
   C. probably the healthier patients took part in the recreation program, and this was the reason for their earlier discharge
   D. recreation was the major determinant of earlier discharge

6.____

7. The one of the following it would be BEST to do when preparing or developing an annual report of a large recreational program is to
   A. gather material such as photos, program descriptions, news stories, and statistics which appeared during the courses of the year
   B. use narrative description rather than charts or graphs to present statistical data
   C. present only the positive aspects and successes of your program, elaborating when necessary to give a favorable picture
   D. give praise to key political figures in the report so they will support the program in the future

7.____

8. *Crash* programs of recreation have sometimes been rushed into slum areas as a response to the threat of violence. Often, the approach has been to present *portable* programs, for example, portable pools put into lots of streets, mobile libraries and nature displays, puppet shows, movies, and rock or soul music shows.
   Of the following, the MAJOR weakness of the *portable* recreation approach is that
   A. funds expended for such programs tend to be excessive and the general public is antagonized
   B. it emphasizes expending aimless energy rather than promoting social growth
   C. it meets only temporary recreation needs and fails to effect a permanent resolution of recreation problems

8.____

D. it tends to draw large numbers of youth out on the street, where they become riotous

9. A recent change in the concept of recreation as a public service is that it is now being thought of as a kind of social therapy.
   The MOST recent illustration of this has been the
   A. joint effort of religious agencies to develop new recreation programs, including year-round camping, for broken families
   B. expanded recreation programs in youth houses, remand institutions, and similar institutions run by the Department of Social Services
   C. new recreation program in private or multi-room occupancy hotels
   D. crash effort to provide recreation programs for alcoholics and older drug addicts

9._____

10. Low-income and racial minority youth tend to have very limited recreation interests. Often, teenage boys want to take part in basketball, but little else of an organized nature.
    For a recreation center director, what would be the BEST professional approach to this attitude?
    A. Begin with the interests they already have, then try to broaden their involvement in other recreation, athletic, or cultural activities
    B. Stick to basketball, their true interest, since they resist other activities
    C. Since they are able to play basketball in many neighborhood settings, eliminate this part of the program and offer new kinds of sports, cultural activities, and social events
    D. Rely on carefully prepared interest survey, and then offer youth only the activities and events they say they want

10._____

11. A NEW trend in many cities, with respect to the assignment of recreation leadership personnel, is to
    A. assign workers to one setting on a full-time, year-round basis so that they will be completely familiar with the work and do a superior job
    B. use seniority more than ever before, thereby giving the long-time employee freedom to pick his job
    C. rotate the assignments of workers from season-to-season or even day-to-day maximize output and improve morale by giving challenging assignments
    D. create new job shifts, such as one week from 9:00 to 5:00, next week from 2:00 to 10:00, etc.

11._____

12. Recreation counseling is becoming more widely used in many hospitals. Such counseling is PRIMARILY intended to
    A. help patients explore their leisure attitudes and interests and motivate them toward fuller participation after discharge
    B. teach patients a broad range of activities, such as sports, crafts, and social skills, that they can use after discharge
    C. use the recreation situation to uncover problems that can then be discussed when the patient gets therapeutic counseling

12._____

D. allow the patients to advise staff members on how best to organize the recreation program

13. A major problem today in many recreation and park departments is costly and destructive vandalism.
Which of the following methods of dealing with this problem has NOT been widely accepted throughout the United States?
   A. Provide stronger enforcement of rules and better surveillance and protection of recreation and park facilities
   B. Offer more attractive programs since people are less likely to vandalize a facility if it is staffed and providing popular community activities
   C. Use new types of designs so that facilities are less prone to vandalism, such as windowless buildings, concrete benches and tables, etc.
   D. Abandon parks or playgrounds that have been repeatedly vandalized

13.____

14. The Board of Education has a strong commitment to recreation.
Its recreation program focuses CHIEFLY on
   A. adult education programs in adult centers
   B. children and youth in after-school and evening centers
   C. the categories of pre-school, mentally handicapped, and senior citizens
   D. youth either considered to be pre-delinquent or adjudicated as delinquent

14.____

15. Those working to provide recreation to persons who have a physical, mental, emotional, or social disability frequently seek assistance from social service agencies.
Which of the following pairs of agencies is LEAST likely to be helpful to them?
   A. Catholic Charities; Federation of Protestant Welfare Agencies
   B. United Cerebral Palsy of N.Y.C.; New York Association for the Blind
   C. New York Association for Retarded Children; National Wheelchair Athletic Association
   D. New York League for Crippled and Disabled Children, Adults and Aging; Handclasp for the Handicapped, Inc.

15.____

16. Throughout the nation, there has been an increase in senior centers for aging persons.
Which of the following agencies does NOT sponsor special centers for aging persons?
   A. Housing Authority's low-income projects
   B. Office of Continuing Education
   C. Parks, Recreation and Cultural Affairs Administration
   D. Department of Social Services

16.____

17. The municipal department that has the PRIMARY responsibility for providing social services for youth, including recreation, is the
   A. Youth Activities Board
   B. Youth Services Agency
   C. United Block Association for Youth
   D. Bureau of Youth Community Services

17.____

18. If a recreation center director had severe problems with drug users in his neighborhood, the APPROPRIATE municipal department for him to ask for assistance is the
    A. Health and Hospitals Corporation
    B. Syanon or Phoenix House
    C. Department of Correction
    D. Addiction Services Agency

18.____

Questions 19-20.

DIRECTIONS: Questions 19 and 20 are to be answered SOLELY on the basis of the following passage.

This country was built on the puritanical belief that honest toil was the foundation of moral rectitude, the cement of society, and the uphill road to progress. Idleness was sin. As a result, we treat free time today as a conditional joy. We permit ourselves to relax only as a reward for hard work or as the recreation needed to put us back into shape for the job. Thus, the aimless delightful play of children gives way in adult life to a serious dedication to golf, the game that is so good for business.

19. According to the above passage, during former times in this country, respectable work was considered to be MOST NEARLY a
    A. way to improve health
    B. form of recreation
    C. developer of good character
    D. reward for leisure

19.____

20. According to the point of view presented in the above passage, it would be MOST reasonable to assume that an employer would consider an employee's vacation to be a time for the employee to
    A. determine his own leisure time priorities
    B. loaf and relax
    C. learn new recreational skills
    D. increase his effectiveness at work

20.____

Questions 21-23.

DIRECTIONS: Questions 21 through 23 are to be answered SOLELY on the basis of the following passage.

One of the key supervisory problems in a large municipal recreation department is that many leaders are assigned to isolated playgrounds or small centers, where it is difficult to observe their work regularly. Often their facilities are extremely limited. In such settings, as well as in larger recreation centers, where many recreation leaders tend to have other jobs as well, there tends to be a low level of morale and incentive. Still, it is the supervisor's task to help recreation personnel to develop pride in their work, and to maintain a high level of performance. With isolated leaders, the supervisor may give advice or assistance. Leaders may be assigned to different tasks or settings during the year to maximize their productivity and provide new challenges. When it is clear that leaders are not willing to make a real effort to contribute to the department, the possibility of penalties must be considered, within the scope of departmental policy and the union contract. However, the supervisor should be constructive, encourage and assist workers to take a greater interest in their work, be innovative, and try to raise morale and to improve performance in positive ways.

21. The one of the following that would be the MOST appropriate title for the foregoing passage is
    A. SMALL COMMUNITY CENTERS – PRO AND CON
    B. PLANNING BETTER RECREATION PROGRAMS
    C. THE SUPERVISOR'S TASK IN UPGRADING PERSONNEL PERFORMANCE
    D. THE SUPERVISOR AND THE MUNICIPAL UNION – RIGHTS AND OBLIGATIONS

21.____

22. The above passage makes clear that recreation leadership performance in ALL recreation playgrounds and centers throughout a large city is
    A. generally above average, with good morale on the part of most recreation leaders
    B. beyond description since no one has ever observed or evaluated leaders
    C. a key test of the personnel department's effort to develop more effective hiring standards
    D. of mixed quality, with many recreation leaders having poor morale and a low level of achievement

22.____

23. According to the above passage, the supervisor's role is to
    A. use disciplinary action as his major tool in upgrading performance
    B. tolerate the lack of effort of individual employees since they are assigned to isolated playgrounds or small centers
    C. employ encouragement, advice, and, when appropriate, disciplinary action to improve performance
    D. inform the county supervisor whenever malfeasance or idleness is detected

23.____

Questions 24-25.

DIRECTIONS: Questions 24 and 25 are to be answered SOLELY on the basis of the following passage.

A recent study revealed some very concrete evidence concerning the relationship between avocations and mental health. A number of well-adjusted persons were surveyed as to the type, number, and duration of their hobbies. The findings were compared to those from a similar survey of mentally disturbed persons. In the well-adjusted group, both the number of hobbies and the intensity with which they were pursued were far greater than that of the mentally disturbed group.

24. According to the above passage, the study showed that
    A. well-adjusted people engage in hobbies more widely and deeply than do mentally disturbed people
    B. hobbies, if taken seriously, serve to keep most people mentally well

24.____

C. mental patients should be taught hobbies as a part of their therapy
D. the degree of interest in hobbies plays an important role in maintaining good mental health

25. In reference to the study mentioned in the above passage, it is MOST accurate to say that it appears to have 25._____
    A. been based on a carefully-structured, complex research design
    B. considered the variables of mental health and hobby involvement
    C. contained a general definition of mental health
    D. given evidence of a causal relationship between hobbies and mental health

---

KEY (CORRECT ANSWERS)

1.	D		11.	C
2.	A		12.	A
3.	A		13.	D
4.	D		14.	B
5.	D		15.	D
6.	B		16.	B
7.	A		17.	B
8.	C		18.	D
9.	B		19.	C
10.	A		20.	D

21.	C
22.	D
23.	C
24.	A
25.	B

EXAMINATION SECTION
TEST 1

DIRECTIONS: Each question or incomplete statement is followed by several suggested answers or completions. Select the one that BEST answers the question or completes the statement. *PRINT THE LETTER OF THE CORRECT ANSWER IN THE SPACE AT THE RIGHT.*

1. The _____ goals of a park and recreation department consist of those outcomes the agency seeks to achieve by offering programs.

    A. external
    B. adaptation
    C. positional
    D. management

    1.____

2. Most recreation professionals would include each of the following in a definition of *recreation* EXCEPT

    A. requiring personal and free choice on the part of the recreationist
    B. requiring a commitment by the recreationist
    C. rewarding insofar as the recreationist can establish and meet certain specific goals
    D. occurring during nonobligated time

    2.____

3. For what type of bond is a *sinkable* fund generally used?

    A. Callable
    B. Serial
    C. Assessment
    D. Term

    3.____

4. Which of the following would be involved in an assessment of a manager's socioemotional skills?

    A. Efficiency orientation
    B. Self-control
    C. Conceptualization
    D. Logical thought

    4.____

5. Which of the following is NOT a typical guideline to be used in community recreation programming?

    A. Community recreation should meet significant social needs.
    B. Special groups in the community, such as the mentally or physically disabled, should be served by recreation programs that meet their social, emotional, creative, and physical needs.
    C. Recreational activities should involve fixed schedules, locations, and personnel that commumity members will be able to rely upon and schedule around with few surprises.
    D. Community recreation programs should be meaningfully interpreted to the public at large through effective public relations media and community relations activities.

    5.____

6. The maintenance department of a park and recreation agency should maintain a workload file containing all copies of submitted forms. Which of the following is NOT a convincing reason for this?

    A. Workers often forget their assignments.
    B. The completed tasks reveal a dollar value useful during budgeting.

    6.____

21

C. Originals may get lost.
D. A special request for priority consideration be made if delays jeopardize safety or morale.

7. As part of an overall effort to reduce costs, park and recreation departments are likely to decrease expenditures related to budget items such as each of the following EXCEPT

    A. gasoline consumption and number of vehicles in department pools
    B. purchase of consumable supplies (paper, paint, crayons, basketballs, etc.) that are dispensed to the public without fee or accountability
    C. special programs that are seasonal or infrequently scheduled
    D. subscriptions, memberships, and purchase of books and training films

8. The National Recreation and Park Association recommends that if a public swimming pool is built for a community, it provide _____ square feet of swimming area of every 1% to 3% of the community population.

    A. 5 B. 15 C. 25 D. 40

9. According to surveys of park and recreation employees at the non-managerial level, the MOST important motivating factor for working in the field is

    A. being part of a team and not letting them down
    B. good working conditions
    C. doing work that is perceived by the employee to be important and worthwhile
    D. appreciation by supervisors for work performed

10. In programming recreational sports contests or tournaments, a department sometimes declines to take complete responsibility for scheduling, and relies instead on a system of *instant* scheduling. Each of the following is an advantage associated with this system EXCEPT

    A. it encourages entries well before the final deadline
    B. participants do not need to be contacted until playoff time, unless there is a schedule change
    C. there is no need for a large physical setting to conduct the process for large numbers of people
    D. selection of alternate playing times is done by participants

11. The _____ budget represents a combination of the object and function classification methods.

    A. performance
    B. classification by fund
    C. classification by organizational units
    D. operating

12. In budget planning sessions, a diagraph can be used to provide information about each of the following EXCEPT

    A. areas of needed program service
    B. months of greatest and least congestion
    C. geographical relations between major facilities
    D. conflicts among special events

13. A summer camp program includes rigidly planned meals, a rising hour, and bedtime, but other phases of the program are planned by both counselors and campers. This program could best be described as

    A. totally nonstructured
    B. having a skeletal structure
    C. semistructured
    D. fully structured

14. Typically, policymaking in public agencies is determined by each of the following EXCEPT

    A. departmental factors
    B. recommendations of professional societies
    C. recommendations of clientele
    D. professional literature

15. Which of the following is considered to be the responsibility of a program staff member at a park and recreation department?

    A. Attending to equipment
    B. Supervising a playground
    C. Monitoring the operating budget
    D. Helping plan policies and procedures

16. It is generally NOT a purpose of a public park and recreation department's public relations efforts to

    A. attempt to coordinate the actions and attitudes of the public and the organization that seeks to serve it
    B. disseminate information to the public
    C. alter the public's beliefs and actions through persuasion
    D. parry the negative efforts of political foes within the municipality or region

17. In deciding whether or not to engage in a certain recreational activity, which of the following steps would a person typically assess FIRST?

    A. His or her own personal suitability to the activity
    B. The probability that participation actually will result in possible benefits
    C. The relative value of the activity
    D. The feasibility of participating

18. A public park and recreation agency's most commonly exercised method of acquiring property for facilities is to

    A. secure an easement
    B. transfer lands or exchange properties from one government department to another
    C. compel subdividers into setting aside property for recreational and park use
    D. purchase the property directly from its owner

19. In most litigation involving park and recreation departments, which of the following is LEAST likely to be the target of litigious action?

    A. The program sponsor
    B. Administrators or supervisors
    C. The employee whose conduct is a direct or proximate cause of the injury
    D. A volunteer serving as an administrative adviser

20. After recreation programs have been initially planned and presented, each of the following concepts will be useful to consider in making program modifications EXCEPT

    A. required facilities
    B. program life cycle
    C. methods of program presentation
    D. program structure and degree of centralization

21. With which of the following statements, about the unionization of park and recreation workers, would an agency head most likely DISAGREE? It has

    A. improved the welfare of the employees by gaining for them higher salaries and benefits than they would have otherwise received
    B. enhanced the organization's ability to offer programs and services on the days and at the times when they are most desired by the public
    C. enhanced management's ability to hire well-qualified personnel
    D. forced the organization to reduce the quantity of services it provides for the public

22. Which of the following is NOT likely to be included in the land records of a park and recreation department?

    A. Where the official deeds are filed
    B. Official actions affecting the title such as street vacations, etc.
    C. Non-liability insurance records
    D. Legal description of the land

23. A manager responds to an employee's grievance by saying he feels sorry for the employee, but cannot do anything to change the situation. The manager has offered a(n) _____ response.

    A. situational   B. sympathetic
    C. judgmental   D. empathetic

24. In a working environment involving a mature group, the leader defines what is to be done, but engages also in supporting behavior intended to contribute to the group's willingness to work at a task. According to situational leadership theory, this mode of leadership is called

    A. participating   B. telling
    C. selling   D. delegating

25. For a large organization such as a park and recreation department, the MOST important aspect of maintaining financial controls is/are
    A. keeping adequate financial records and preparing and submitting monthly reports relating expenditures to categories in the annual budget
    B. establishing and enforcing strict cost control procedures
    C. the department's procedures for purchasing supplies or equipment
    D. the department's procedural requirements for making and enforcing contractual agreements

KEY (CORRECT ANSWERS)

1. A
2. C
3. D
4. B
5. C

6. A
7. C
8. B
9. C
10. C

11. A
12. C
13. B
14. C
15. C

16. D
17. C
18. D
19. D
20. A

21. B
22. C
23. B
24. C
25. A

TEST 2

DIRECTIONS: Each question or incomplete statement is followed by several suggested answers or completions. Select the one that BEST answers the question or completes the statement. *PRINT THE LETTER OF THE CORRECT ANSWER IN THE SPACE AT THE RIGHT.*

1. Each of the following is a type of supervisory board or commission associated with public recreation and park departments EXCEPT

   A. semi-independent bodies with the power to make policy, but dependent on a higher governmental body that provides funding and to which they must report
   B. advisory boards or commissions with limited powers
   C. completely independent bodies with full authority for establishing and overseeing policy
   D. independent bodies which do not make policy, but are primarily responsible for locating and distributing funds associated with policies formulated by another body

2. Which of the following is NOT a key managerial function in the process of organizing?

   A. Determination of recruitment and hiring policies
   B. Defining goals and objectives
   C. Clustering functions within the organization
   D. Assigning responsibility to individuals and granting authority

3. The authority for raising taxes and spending money for municipal recreation services comes from

   A. state legislatures
   B. the local board
   C. local elections
   D. the welfare clauses of the Constitution

4. Studies in public parks and recreation departments have shown that although the public shows initial resistance to the imposition of new or increased fees for use of programs, services, and facilities, the short-term decline in usage tends to disappear within

   A. 6-8 months
   B. 12-18 months
   C. 2-3 years
   D. 3-5 years

5. For legal purposes, the standard of care owed to a user by a park and recreation department is determined by classifying the types of users into three broad categories. Which of the following is NOT one of these categories?

   A. Licensee
   B. Trespasser
   C. Invitee
   D. Grantee

6. The primary *disadvantage* associated with the use of a double-elimination format for scheduled recreational tournaments is that

   A. it does not tend to hold the interest of participants
   B. the format is often confusing for participants to follow
   C. it is perceived as being unfair
   D. it does not allow a participant to have an *off day*

7. When estimating the short-term recreational facility demand projections for a community, a manager should describe the agency's actions to be taken over the next _____ years.

    A. 1-2   B. 3-5   C. 5-10   D. 15

8. If the existence of an *attractive nuisance* can be proved, a park and recreation department can be found liable for an injury to a person who has illegally trespassed onto an unsupervised facility.
   Each of the following conditions is necessary in order to prove the existence of an *attractive nuisance* EXCEPT

    A. the trespasser is a child who is judged to be too young to know better
    B. the property is not completely enclosed by a fence at least 6 feet in height
    C. the agency or owner of the land upon which the child trespasses is aware that the area is attractive to children
    D. a dangerous condition exists on the property that is not a natural hazard

9. Within a working group, the degree to which a situation is favorable or unfavorable for the use of a task-oriented leadership style is MOST dependent on

    A. the quality of leader-member relationships
    B. task structure
    C. the size of the group
    D. the leader's position power

10. A park and recreation department leases a golf course to another agency. In terms of liability, the department is practicing risk

    A. avoidance   B. reduction
    C. transfer   D. retention

11. Cost accounting is useful to a park and recreation department in each of the following ways EXCEPT

    A. determining the proper balance between different phases of departmental operation
    B. evaluating individual personnel performance
    C. evaluating expenditures referenced to different elements of the community population
    D. determining the feasibility of constructing facilities with either the agency's own labor or on a contractual basis

12. The contract method of scheduling personnel in a park and recreation department is unrealistic when

    A. positions require specialization
    B. personnel qualifications and availability are consistent
    C. employees wish to select their own days and shifts
    D. the system requires the establishment of work schedules for a specific time span

13. In the personnel classification system traditionally used in public agencies such as park and recreation departments, supervisors are normally responsible for

    A. coordinating and directing the overall work of the department
    B. overseeing responsibilities within a geographical area or district of a community

C. planning, organizing, and directly supervising recreation programs in one or more facilities
D. recruiting, selecting, assigning, and supervising all department personnel

14. Which of the following steps in a municipal park planning procedure is generally performed FIRST?

    A. The preliminary design
    B. Inspection of the site with topographic map in hand
    C. The making of the investigative report
    D. Working drawings and specifications

15. When a manager or supervisor relies upon a(n) _____ style of leadership, the reaction of employees will most often be hostility and aggression within members of the group.

    A. laissez-faire   B. democratic
    C. authoritative   D. autocratic

16. Which of the following approaches to recreation program development is focused on the need to provide programs that are responsive to community pressures and influences?

    A. Traditional   B. Expressed desires
    C. Sociopolitical   D. Current practices

17. Risk retention is a valid policy for a park and recreation department under each of the following conditions EXCEPT when

    A. the maximum possible loss is so small that the agency can absorb it in the operating budget
    B. it is possible to transfer the risks to another
    C. the probability of a loss is so low that it can be ignored
    D. the cost to transfer the risk is so high that it would cost almost as much as the worst loss that could occur

18. Most public park and recreation department contracts with other organizations fall into several clearly defined categories. Which of the following is LEAST likely to be one of these?

    A. Direct programming and leadership of department services
    B. The purchase of equipment, materials, and supplies
    C. Planning, design, or construction of capital facilities
    D. Arrangements for concessions, franchises, or leases of special types of service or facilities

19. To make an agency's services more effective, supervision of staff should be thought of as a(n) _____ process.

    A. permissive   B. directing
    C. enabling   D. controlling

20. Which type of commercial leisure-service organizations account for the greatest dollar-volume of annual sales?

    A. Partnerships   B. Institutions
    C. Corporations   D. Sole proprietorships

21. In addition to public resistance to the implementation of a fee structure for certain services or facilities, a park and recreation department may encounter some administrative problems. Which of the following is NOT typically one of these problems?

    A. The fees may be illegal in some cases
    B. Difficulty in controlling access to services where fees are levied
    C. The exclusion of certain disadvantaged groups may present an unmanageable apparatus
    D. The cost of administering fees may be more than the revenues generated by it

22. When composing a grant proposal, which of the following pieces of information will probably be LEAST useful to the reader?

    A. Demonstration of critical need
    B. Capital facilities that can be used as collateral
    C. A precise statement of the budget
    D. Availability of matching funds

23. To be most effective in his or her leadership role, a manager in a park and recreation department should be each of the following EXCEPT

    A. optimistic
    B. aggressive
    C. resilient
    D. reactive

24. Recreation and park administrators should involve themselves as fully as possible in each construction project — according to each of the following guidelines EXCEPT

    A. become familiar with all background information related to the facility plan and be actively involved in all public hearings
    B. be present at the first design conference to make sure program needs are considered, and then obtaining a summary of each modification session
    C. insist that all construction details or standards be carried out exactly as specified
    D. visit the construction site regularly, once construction begins, either with staff members or with the architect

25. Volunteers at a park and recreation department are LEAST likely to assist in

    A. the budgeting process
    B. program delivery
    C. logistical services
    D. an administrative-advisory capacity

KEY (CORRECT ANSWERS)

1. D
2. A
3. D
4. C
5. D
6. B
7. B
8. B
9. A
10. C

11. C
12. A
13. B
14. C
15. D
16. C
17. B
18. A
19. C
20. C

21. C
22. B
23. D
24. B
25. A

EXAMINATION SECTION
TEST 1

DIRECTIONS: Each question or incomplete statement is followed by several suggested answers or completions. Select the one that BEST answers the question or completes the statement. *PRINT THE LETTER OF THE CORRECT ANSWER IN THE SPACE AT THE RIGHT.*

1. A well-conceived and effectively presented budget should do each of the following EXCEPT

    A. inform taxpayers and government officials of the amounts of money spent, the sources of revenue, and the costs of achieving departmental goals
    B. serve for evaluating the program and ensuring that objectives are met
    C. help in promoting flexible operational procedures by creating very few classifications for all expenditures, and requiring flexible procedures for approving them
    D. provide a general statement of the financial needs, resources, and plans of the department, including an outline of all program elements and their costs and allocations for facilities and personnel

2. Among volunteers who offer time to park and recreation departments, which of the following motivating factors is most prevalent?

    A. Preparation for paid employment
    B. Family influences
    C. A desire to feel needed
    D. A desire to be helpful

3. Which of the following approaches to leisure service is found chiefly among recreation and park managers who serve in resource-based agencies?

    A. Individualist
    B. Prescriptive
    C. Environmental/aesthetic
    D. Human-services

4. In most public park and recreation departments, the largest area of use for volunteer workers is in

    A. direct leadership of groups or assisting professional leaders at work
    B. specialized educational appointments
    C. clerical assistance and helping with mailings, reports, and similar assignments
    D. administrative, promotional, or advisory activities

5. The use of night lighting at outdoor recreational facilities typically creates each of the following benefits EXCEPT

    A. deterring personal crime
    B. overall lower cost per hour of public use
    C. beautification of the park by enhancing plants, trees, and architectural features
    D. distinguishing activities within the park

6. Of the four types of in-service training administered to entry-level park and recreation employees, which is most likely to be delivered on an individual basis?

A. General career development
B. Training to keep the worker up to date
C. Orientation to the job
D. Training related specifically to the position for which the employee was selected

7. In recent years, community leisure-service organizations have adopted each of the following methods for achieving a high degree of productivity and efficiency EXCEPT

    A. cost-cutting practices
    B. zero-based budgeting
    C. a more extensive use of cost-benefit analysis
    D. reduced contracting, concession, and leasing arrangements

8. Which of the following statements concerning contributory negligence and children is TRUE?
   A child
    I. under 7 years of age is conclusively adjudged to be incapable of contributory negligence
    II. between 7 and 10 years of age is rebuttably presumed to be incapable of negligence
    III. over fourteen years of age is presumed capable of negligence
   The CORRECT answer is:

    A. I only   B. I, II   C. I, III   D. II, III

9. In general, a daily program schedule is divided into blocks of time, with major blocks of time of an hour or more per block incorporated. Generally, the daily program schedule is arranged with

    A. one block of time scheduled in the morning and one in the afternoon
    B. one in the morning and two in the afternoon
    C. only one major block per day, usually in the morning
    D. only one major block per day, usually in the afternoon

10. The MAIN advantage of an unstructured, decentralized approach to recreational programming is

    A. being able to respond to local neighborhood needs and special characteristics
    B. a set of core activities that meet clear program guidelines
    C. more intimate contact between community members and recreational leaders
    D. more efficient use of personnel resources

11. According to the Management-by-Objectives model (MBO), which of the following is NOT a guideline for the setting of park and recreation agency objectives?

    A. Objectives must be broad and open to interpretation by evaluators.
    B. Personnel at each level should play a role in setting their own objectives.
    C. A limited number of major objectives should be used for each unit or individual.
    D. Each objective should be given a precise time limit for accomplishment.

12. Which of the following steps in the purchasing process of a public agency would typically occur FIRST? 12.____

    A. Justification
    B. Bids
    C. Specifications
    D. Purchase orders

13. Of the various types of fees and charges at their disposal, public recreation and park departments most often use 13.____

    A. entrance/admission fees
    B. lease revenue
    C. program/activity fees
    D. rental fees

14. When a park and recreation official has the opportunity to speak with the media about the operations of the department, he or she should 14.____

    A. speak in 30-second quotes, or shorter
    B. use technical language that will show the significance of the project or organization
    C. dress in bright colors
    D. use preface remarks

15. Each of the following is an advantage associated with contracting out various functions of a public park and recreation department EXCEPT 15.____

    A. greater departmental independence
    B. avoiding the restrictions of bureaucratic structures and similar political institutions
    C. lower personnel costs
    D. clearer contractual specification of quantity, quality, and price of work

16. Which of the following is NOT a growing trend in the personnel assignment policies of larger park and recreation departments? 16.____

    A. Having a fixed number of full-time, year-round employees supplemented by a limited number of specialists during the year, and an influx of summer workers for playground or camping programs
    B. Greater responsibility of *face-to-face* leaders in coordinating and directing programs
    C. Assignment of leaders to other district- or city-wide roles which can be carried out during slack periods
    D. Rotation of assignments at different seasons

17. According to most current practices in public agencies, the first work sessions on the departmental budget for the following year are generally held in the months of 17.____

    A. March-April
    B. May-June
    C. August-September
    D. October-November

18. Which of the following appears to have the LEAST significant effect on a person's opportunities to engage in recreational activities? 18.____

    A. Time
    B. Geographic and environmental resources
    C. Motivation
    D. Health and fitness

19. A park and recreation department's _____ is a document that includes planned and proposed expenditures for carrying out major purchases and construction projects of a substantial and long-term nature.

    A. operating budget
    B. balance sheet
    C. capital budget
    D. performance budget

20. A large park of several hundred acres will generally provide _____ acres of area for every user.

    A. 1-2   B. 5   C. 10   D. 20

21. Concerning intramural and extramural sports programs, most park and recreation departments have specific policies designed to deal with the issue of forfeited contests. Which of the following is NOT generally one of these policies?

    A. A team or individual not ready to play within thirty minutes after the scheduled time is charged with a forfeit.
    B. An individual or team may be assessed a forfeit fee.
    C. Two forfeits result in the elimination of an individual or team from all further participation in that sport.
    D. If a team or individual leaves before the forfeit is duly noted by an official or supervisor, then both teams should be charged with a forfeit.

22. Most local park and recreation agencies function within a framework of legislation provided by the

    A. federal government
    B. state government
    C. municipal government
    D. appointed board

23. Within a working group assigned to a specific task, the task structure is measured by each of the following EXCEPT the degree to which

    A. members understand what the goal is
    B. the correctness of a decision can be demonstrated by authority or logic
    C. multiple paths to the goal are evident
    D. one solution is more correct

24. During a summer recreation program, quiet activities are usually BEST scheduled for

    A. as late in the day as possible
    B. the early afternoon
    C. mid-day
    D. the early morning

25. Which of the following statements about adolescent recreationists is FALSE?

    A. They generally show a rapid increase in lung capacity.
    B. They are capable not only of describing, but of explaining situations or phenomena.
    C. Norms for male or female behavior are generally discovered through interactions with the opposite sex.
    D. They are concerned with the meaning of life according to religious and philosophical perspectives.

KEY (CORRECT ANSWERS)

1.	C	11.	A
2.	D	12.	A
3.	C	13.	C
4.	A	14.	A
5.	B	15.	A
6.	C	16.	A
7.	D	17.	B
8.	C	18.	C
9.	B	19.	C
10.	A	20.	B

21. A
22. B
23. C
24. C
25. C

TEST 2

DIRECTIONS: Each question or incomplete statement is followed by several suggested answers or completions. Select the one that BEST answers the question or completes the statement. *PRINT THE LETTER OF THE CORRECT ANSWER IN THE SPACE AT THE RIGHT.*

1. In developing any recreation program, an administrator's primary emphasis is nearly always on

    A. education for leisure
    B. providing organized or supervised activities
    C. coordinating and assisting functions
    D. providing facilities for unscheduled and unsupervised use

1.____

2. Each of the following is a disadvantage associated with the use of air-supported structures as a housing for recreational facilities EXCEPT

    A. their susceptibility to vandalism
    B. their short life expectancy
    C. lack of flexibility in yearly program scheduling
    D. possible zoning law conflicts

2.____

3. Typically, which of the following would be the final step in the development of a maintenance management plan for a recreational facility?
The

    A. definition of the maintenance plan's overall goals and objectives
    B. development of work order request forms for non-routine, nonrecurring maintenance tasks
    C. creation of a format for scheduling maintenance work
    D. development of a form for daily maintenance work and assignments

3.____

4. In liability terms, each of the following is a means of risk reduction for a park and recreation department EXCEPT

    A. conducting periodic safety inspections for all facilities and equipment
    B. training all employees in safety practices, first aid, and preventive maintenance
    C. clearly labeling potential risks to users
    D. developing safety rules for the operation of facilities and equipment

4.____

5. Managing a public park and recreation department like a business, using marketing strategies, has proven effective for many departments in trimming costs and streamlining services, but the marketing approach does have several disadvantages. Which of the following is NOT generally considered to be one of them?

    A. The bottom line of program development is profitability.
    B. Efforts at securing public subsidies are likely to be reduced.
    C. Services to poorer community residents may atrophy.
    D. Possible ventures may be evaluated only in terms of who will be able to pay for them.

5.____

6. The need for public relations in the field of parks and recreation is enforced by certain prevailing public attitudes. Which of the following is NOT generally considered to be one of these prevailing attitudes?

   A. Frequent occasions, brought about by the very nature of park and recreation operations, when individual citizens become irritated, frustrated, or disappointed
   B. Limited knowledge of the range of services and programs offered
   C. A generalized opposition to public funding of a department that is not considered to be part of the infrastructure
   D. The feeling that public recreation is not really a necessity; that the public is able to meet its leisure needs independently

7. In most states, the statute of limitations for litigating actions involving negligence is

   A. 1 year
   B. 2 years
   C. 10 years
   D. in most states, there is no statute of limitations

8. In park and recreation management applications, a *diagraph* is used to

   A. view the community-wide availability of programs and detect under- or over-provision of different types of activities on a geographical basis
   B. show all events or continuing activities in a convenient and easily understood form
   C. show individual projects or programs laid out along a calendar, with specific tasks indicated for the dates on which they are to be begun and completed
   D. identify major facilities and ongoing programs

9. Which of the following is considered to be the responsibility of a program-administrative staff member at a park and recreation department?

   A. Monitoring personnel practices
   B. Preparing statistical or analytical reports of operations
   C. Monitoring facility use and operations
   D. Implementing policies for safety

10. The probationary period for most newly-hired park and recreation personnel is

    A. 24-48 hours
    B. 4-6 weeks
    C. 3-6 months
    D. 1-2 years

11. For busy community members who have fluctuating schedules, and who want to compete in a more structured competitive environment, a recreation and park department's most effective way of dealing with competitive sports such as tennis is to establish a _____ tournament structure for participants.

    A. single elimination
    B. double elimination
    C. challenge
    D. round-robin

12. A specific tax leveled against the assessed value of residential or industrial property, the amount of which is assigned directly to the public park and recreation fund and used exclusively for that purpose, is known as a(n) _____ tax.

    A. millage
    B. real estate
    C. impact
    D. levy

13. A _____ approach to leisure service sees recreation not as an activity carried on for its own sake, but as designed to accomplish specific therapeutic goals.

    A. human-services B. marketing
    C. individualist D. prescriptive

14. Which of the following steps in the development of a park and recreation program is typically administered first?

    A. Establishing goals, objectives, and policies
    B. Identifying the range of possible activities and services
    C. Assessing participant or community needs and interests
    D. Developing a program plan

15. The growing trend in park and recreation departmental budgeting is toward the use of _____ budgets.

    A. program B. function classification
    C. performance D. line-item

16. What type of accounting system shows, on updated expenditure reports, all encumbrances or charges against specified accounts?

    A. Balance sheet B. Concurrent auditing
    C. Work program auditing D. Accrual

17. Which of the following statements about recreationists in middle childhood (6-12 years) is generally TRUE?

    A. Their muscles develop in function, but are still immature in size and strength.
    B. They have not mastered the concept of numbers, clock time, or calendar time.
    C. They do not exhibit abstract thought processes.
    D. They know rules which specify right from wrong, but may not understand the reasoning behind them.

18. Which of the following is NOT a typical benefit associated with informal structures and processes within the framework of a park and recreation department?

    A. Enhancement of a manager's authority
    B. Reduced time requirements for developing projects
    C. Increased opportunity for lower-level personnel to share meaningfully in agency planning
    D. Improved planning and problem-solving functions

19. Which of the following administration philosophies or strategies is NOT part of the future-oriented trend in park and recreation management?

    A. Evaluating services in terms of human consequences
    B. Offering programs anywhere in the community, with staff resources helping residents develop their own leadership skills
    C. Funding all basic programs from tax allocations
    D. Acting in an enabling or catalyzing role in matching community resources to citizen's needs

20. When a recreation and park manager has news of interest to the local newspaper, there are several approaches he or she might take. Which of the following should be used most sparingly?

    A. Arranging a news conference and invite interested reporters and editors
    B. Calling the newspaper, summarizing the information briefly to the appropriate editor or reporter, and allowing the person to suggest a course of action
    C. Writing the information in the form of a *letter to the editor* and mail or deliver it to the editor
    D. Preparing a news release and mail or deliver it to the editor

21. Each of the following is a typical policy used by park and recreation departments concerning the reservation of recreational facilities by community members EXCEPT

    A. cancellations must be made in person with the proper identification
    B. cancellations must be made 24 hours in advance, or a no-show penalty will apply
    C. persons absent 10 minutes past the reserved time forfeit all rights to the facility
    D. reservations must be made at least 4 hours in advance

22. In a departmental budget, the function of a work program is *primarily* to

    A. determine scheduling needs for the coming year
    B. estimate personnel expenditures
    C. establish a clear set of administrative performance standards
    D. outline tasks to be performed, standards of service and efficiency, and methods to be used

23. While conducting a needs assessment of the community, park and recreation administrators relate the leisure services currently offered to a set of national standards for such services in similar communities. In this situation, the administration is determining the community's _____ need for services.

    A. expressed   B. normative
    C. perceived   D. relative

24. Which of the following is not typically a heading used on a written maintenance plan for a recreational facility?

    A. Personnel   B. Chain of command
    C. Maintenance standards D. Frequency

25. According to the established national standard, a park and recreation manager who is planning a leisure facility should rely upon the figure of 1 acre of land needed for every _____ community residents.

    A. 100   B. 800   C. 1200   D. 2500

KEY (CORRECT ANSWERS)

1.	D	11.	C
2.	C	12.	A
3.	B	13.	D
4.	C	14.	C
5.	B	15.	A
6.	C	16.	D
7.	B	17.	D
8.	B	18.	A
9.	A	19.	C
10.	C	20.	A

21. D
22. D
23. B
24. B
25. B

EXAMINATION SECTION
TEST 1

DIRECTIONS: Each question or incomplete statement is followed by several suggested answers or completions. Select the one that BEST answers the question or completes the statement. *PRINT THE LETTER OF THE CORRECT ANSWER IN THE SPACE AT THE RIGHT.*

1. For a large public park and recreation department, it is generally agreed that the key to productivity is

   A. contracting and leasing arrangements
   B. the effective management of personnel
   C. cost-benefit analysis
   D. appealing to private foundations for funds

   1.____

2. In a park and recreation setting, four conditions must be present in a situation in order for the department to be found legally negligent, and therefore liable, in the case of an accident. Which of the following is NOT one of these conditions?

   A. Proof of injury or damage
   B. Legal responsibility for the participant
   C. The participant's lack of an employment relationship to the department
   D. The department's failure to take reasonable care

   2.____

3. In a park and recreation department, the MOST effective approach to problem-solving is generally described as

   A. group-centered
   B. authoritarian
   C. decisions by higher authorities
   D. an analysis by planning specialists

   3.____

4. Which of the following administration philosophies or strategies is part of the future-oriented trend in park and recreation management?

   A. Planning programs with the staff, chiefly by updating past programs
   B. Evaluating outcomes primarily through attendance figures
   C. Providing programs and services based on social and economic needs of the community
   D. Requiring financial accountability and justifying budgets based on historical precedent

   4.____

5. The _____ approach to leisure service sees recreation as an important community service that is carried on both for its own sake and because it contributes to the mental and physical health of participants.

   A. human-services   B. prescriptive
   C. environmental   D. quality-of-life

   5.____

6. More or increased _____ is NOT a growing trend in leisure services.

   A. centralized personnel structure
   B. emphasis on health and fitness

   6.____

41

C. consideration of leisure's contribution to quality of life
D. emphasis on noncompetitive forms of play

7. The MOST common means of financing public recreation and park departments is through

   A. bonds
   B. grants
   C. taxes
   D. fees and charges

8. For evaluating the effectiveness of specific programs offered by a park and recreation department, each of the following methods is commonly used EXCEPT

   A. systems-based, goal-achievement models
   B. internal auditing by top management
   C. staff-based evaluation processes
   D. participant-based evaluation

9. A public agency that favors the delegation of authority is BEST described as

   A. heterogeneous
   B. decentralized
   C. individualistic
   D. irresponsible

10. The ability to _____ is NOT generally considered to be a core process that an entry-level employee in a park and recreation department should master.

    A. carry out both program planning and organizational planning
    B. formally articulate resource needs
    C. utilize leadership processes
    D. teach

11. A _____ budget is designed in such a way that large units of work, or special programs, are isolated, identified, and described in detail.

    A. object classification
    B. function classification
    C. program
    D. performance

12. When programming recreational activities for participants in middle childhood (6-12 years), it is important to remember that they are generally

    A. preferring separation into sexually segregated groups
    B. physically aggressive
    C. physically growing more quickly than in preschool years
    D. unconcerned about ideas such as competence, achievement, and approval from others

13. Of the following issues, _____ is LEAST likely to be negotiated in a park and recreation labor union contractual agreement.

    A. work hours
    B. contracting work, or *outsourcing*
    C. safety regulations
    D. retirement plans

14. Which of the following is considered to be the responsibility of an auxiliary staff member at a park and recreation department?

    A. Supervision of sport programs
    B. Monitoring adherence to agency rules
    C. Direction of administrative guidelines
    D. Organizing sport activities

15. Traditionally, leisure facilities have been planned according to

    A. concepts of the neighborhood and community
    B. urban planning methods based on land-use principles
    C. a needs index
    D. recommended standards of open space

16. Public agencies such as park and recreation departments typically use one of several contemporary models in evaluating whether the agency has achieved its stated objectives. Which of the following is NOT one of these models?
    Evaluation designed to measure the

    A. overall quality of programs, based on the opinion of an advisory board
    B. effectiveness of programs in meeting their stated goals and objectives
    C. effectiveness of personnel in carrying out stated program goals and objectives
    D. level of satisfaction of program participants

17. It is NOT typically a function of a public park and recreation agency's board or commission to

    A. review and approve all policies and work with the agency's managers to develop plans for meeting present and future leisure needs of the community
    B. consider and approve all personnel appointments or promotions
    C. articulate to the agency's director and staff how the details of administration should be carried out
    D. carry out long-range planning in cooperation with other community organizations to meet public recreational needs

18. In handling employment inquiries, application forms, and interviews for employment, questions to the applicant about _____ may be allowed under law, whether their use is job-related or not.

    A. employment history
    B. physical requirements
    C. arrest and conviction record
    D. age

19. According to most current practices in public agencies, any overspending or underspending in the year's budget is to be brought to the department head's attention in the month of

    A. January   B. February
    C. March or April   D. November

20. In order to avoid legal liability for certain activities involving children, some park and recreation departments use the convention of permission slips signed by a parent or guardian, in which they are asked to waive the right to sue in case of injury or accident. For several reasons, these slips offer the department a false sense of security. Which of the following is NOT one of these reasons?
    I. In all cases, signed statements are invalid if the risks of the activity are not understood.
    II. The waiver is not valid unless signed by both parents, no matter what their geographic location.
    III. They cannot waive the right of a child to bring suit against the agency when the child reaches the legal age for doing so.

    The CORRECT answer is:

    A. I only B. I, II C. I, III D. I, II, III

21. Which of the following recreation facilities would most likely be located at or near the intersection of major or secondary thoroughfares near the center of a 4- or 5-square mile service area?

    A. Playlot B. Large park
    C. Playground D. Athletic field

22. Which of the following is NOT a level of planning commonly associated with recreation and park facilities?

    A. Planning that focuses solely on recreation and park development within a total community, sometimes as a separate portion of a total plan
    B. Regional planning that takes into account services and facilities offered by adjacent jurisdictions
    C. Planning that is concerned with the development of a particular facility or the needs of a single neighborhood
    D. Total master planning that considers all aspects of municipal growth, including industrial and residential development, transportation, education, housing, health, etc.

23. The MAIN advantage of a structured, centralized approach to recreational programming is

    A. being able to respond to local neighborhood needs
    B. optimum legal protection from liability claims
    C. more efficient use of personnel resources
    D. a set of clear-cut standards for fulfilling the agency's stated objectives

24. When programming recreational activities for participants in middle adulthood (40-65 years), it is important to remember that they generally

    A. experience physiological changes in the brain
    B. begin to experience instability in cognitive skills
    C. display a loss of creativity
    D. tend to gain weight easily

25. In park and recreation accounting, concurrent auditing represents 25._____
    A. a preaudit of expected income or disbursements
    B. a formal check of specific administrative or program divisions of a department, or construction or maintenance projects
    C. a form of bookkeeping report showing the assets and liabilities of a given fund or budget
    D. all departmental expenditures that have been authorized and carried out

---

KEY (CORRECT ANSWERS)

1.	B	11.	C
2.	C	12.	A
3.	A	13.	B
4.	C	14.	A
5.	D	15.	C
6.	A	16.	A
7.	C	17.	C
8.	B	18.	A
9.	B	19.	B
10.	B	20.	C

21.	D
22.	B
23.	D
24.	D
25.	A

TEST 2

DIRECTIONS: Each question or incomplete statement is followed by several suggested answers or completions. Select the one that BEST answers the question or completes the statement. *PRINT THE LETTER OF THE CORRECT ANSWER IN THE SPACE AT THE RIGHT.*

1. Each of the following is a benefit associated with the use of a *matrix* structure in a public park and recreation department EXCEPT   1.____

   A. greater opportunity of employees' personal development
   B. better technical performance
   C. improved flexibility in conditions of change and uncertainty
   D. involvement in long-range planning of employees at every level

2. Which of the following statements about recreationists in early adulthood (20-39 years) is generally TRUE?   2.____

   A. They are more self-centered than adolescents.
   B. Their friendships are characterized by less intimacy.
   C. They experience a lack of stability in intellectual skills.
   D. They expand their social relationships through new contacts within the occupational and community settings.

3. When programming recreation activities, an administrator's choices are likely to be affected by each of the following factors EXCEPT   3.____

   A. the number of potential activities
   B. the characteristics of participants
   C. the funds required
   D. personnel

4. A recreation programmer wants to stage a single-elimination summer softball tournament at the department's facilities. Each of the following is an advantage associated with the single-elimination format EXCEPT it   4.____

   A. is usually more interesting for spectators
   B. may accommodate a large number of participants
   C. encourages maximum participation
   D. is the most economical to conduct

5. In a recreation or park facility's off-season, an administrator wants to maintain a minimum level of care. Typically, how often should litter at the facility be picked up?   5.____

   A. Daily   B. Weekly
   C. Monthly   D. Every two months

6. Funding agencies for public park and recreation departments have historically applied strict criteria for determining grant recipients. Which of the following statements about their considerations is generally FALSE?   6.____

   A. There must be evidence that existing programs and facilities are being fully utilized.
   B. Agencies applying for grants must be prepared to guarantee a substantial portion of the total grant proposal.

C. Higher priority is given to proposals that come from more than one agency or sponsor.
D. Wherever possible, grant proposals should be designed to serve the general population, rather than isolated or special-need communities.

7. In public recreation programs, sport accounts for about _____% of all active involvement.

    A. 10-30   B. 35-50   C. 60-75   D. 80-95

8. Which of the following is NOT a level of responsibility defined by the functional classification of personnel analysis?

    A. Managerial   B. Tutorial
    C. Logistical   D. Operational

9. During a community needs assessment, a park and recreation department would most likely conduct use surveys among the community members in order to determine the _____ leisure needs of the community.

    A. expressed   B. normative   C. relative   D. perceived

10. The main disadvantage to using an *object classification* type of budget for a park and recreation department is that

    A. it does not relate expenditures meaningfully to programs
    B. certain expenditures, such as personnel, are not considered *objects*
    C. it does not provide complete itemization of expenditures
    D. it does not take unplanned expenditures into account

11. Which of the following is NOT a guideline to follow in preparing a newspaper release for a public park and recreation department event or service?

    A. The release should stick to the facts and avoid editorializing.
    B. An attempt should be made to feature a prominent or interesting individual or group of people in the article.
    C. The most important information should be included at the beginning of the article.
    D. The release should be limited to 2 or 3 pages.

12. In a public school or college's recreational facilities, the priority of use must be

    A. intramural or campus recreational programming
    B. intercollegiate practice sessions or competition
    C. formal academic program use
    D. community residents

13. For a supervisor in a park and recreation department, each of the following is a guideline to follow in taking disciplinary action with employees EXCEPT

    A. when correction is required, it should be handled in private
    B. the worker should be told what he or she can do to correct the situation
    C. the action should not be taken until some time after the need for it has been established
    D. take the same corrective actions for the same behaviors with different individuals

14. The healthiest way a park and recreation department manager can approach the subject of inter-employee conflict is to view it as

    A. inevitable, but desirable and able to be used to constructive ends
    B. a healthy sign that workers in the department intend to challenge and compete with one another to meet departmental goals
    C. an inevitable product of a close working relationship that should be not denied, but endured peaceably
    D. a harmful and destructive influence that should be avoided at all costs

15. Which of the following is NOT generally considered to be a guideline to follow in determining when, and for what, recreation fees and charges are justified?

    A. Frequently charge where *preservation* is the dominant function
    B. Be sure that some benefit accrues to the taxpayer
    C. The specific services to be charged for and the fee should be matters of local choice
    D. Frequently charge where *use* is the dominant function

16. Generally, which of the following approaches to urban planning is used LEAST often?

    A. Developing an ideal model of the community
    B. Cost-revenue model
    C. User-oriented approach
    D. Needs index model

17. When conditions within a working group are only moderately favorable or unfavorable (i.e., the leader is well-liked but the task under consideration is unstructured), what type of leadership style is most appropriate?

    A. Laissez-faire   B. Task-oriented
    C. Authoritarian   D. Relationship-oriented

18. In a park and recreation department, a cost-benefit analysis is LEAST likely to be useful for

    A. identifying high- and low-cost programs and services as related to maintenance, administration, and direct leadership costs per participant-hour of service rendered
    B. providing valuable support data for justifying budget requests
    C. providing essential data for determining the cost-effectiveness of individual department personnel
    D. permitting the assignment of priorities to specific programs and services

19. In recent years, the number of volunteers working for public park and recreation departments has increased among certain segments of the population. Among the following groups, which has shown the LEAST significant increase in volunteer service?

    A. Females   B. Males
    C. Poor people   D. Minorities

20. The major type of legislation affecting parks and recreation is the

    A. regulatory law   B. special district law
    C. enabling law   D. home rule legislation

21. When programming recreational activities for participants in late adulthood (over 65 years), it is important to remember that they generally

    A. do not require a significant restructuring of time
    B. have a self-concept that tends to be more dependent upon external factors
    C. prefer to live in close contact with others of their age group
    D. become less active if they are men, and more active if they are women

22. The self-study approach to agency evaluation, outlined by the National Recreation and Park Association, includes standards that are used in measuring the effectiveness of a department in several major categories. Which of the following is NOT one of these categories?

    A. Administration   B. Evaluation
    C. Programming   D. Funding

23. Decisions made at the lower level of an agency's management, which are part of operational planning and program implementation, are described as _____ decisions.

    A. primary   B. problem-oriented
    C. reflex   D. task-oriented

24. In park and recreation applications, a *flowchart* is used to

    A. view the community-wide availability of programs and detect under- or over-provision of different types of activities on a geographical basis
    B. show all events or continuing activities in a convenient and easily understood form
    C. show individual projects or programs laid out along a calendar, with specific tasks indicated for the dates on which they are to be begun and completed
    D. identify major facilities and ongoing programs

25. In recreation and sports injury cases involving parents and children, the parents, but not the child, can be barred from recovery for a child's injury under certain conditions. Which of the following is NOT one of these conditions?
    The

    A. parent has failed to exercise reasonable care to prevent the child from placing himself in a situation in which lack of self-protective capacity may reasonably be expected to result in harm to the child
    B. child is too young to exercise self-protection
    C. child's incapacity is a contributing factor in harm
    D. injury involves an *attractive nuisance*

KEY (CORRECT ANSWERS)

1. D
2. D
3. A
4. C
5. A

6. D
7. C
8. B
9. D
10. A

11. D
12. C
13. C
14. A
15. A

16. B
17. D
18. C
19. A
20. C

21. D
22. D
23. D
24. C
25. D

EXAMINATION SECTION
TEST 1

DIRECTIONS: Each question or incomplete statement is followed by several suggested answers or completions. Select the one that BEST answers the question or completes the statement. *PRINT THE LETTER OF THE CORRECT ANSWER IN THE SPACE AT THE RIGHT.*

1. Assume that the ticket agent at the bathhouse cannot dispense tickets from his machine because of a mechanical failure.
   You should authorize the ticket agent to   1.____

   A. sell tickets by hand from the bundle only
   B. stop selling tickets and await the installation of a stand-by machine
   C. collect cash from the patrons and have them escorted through the bathhouse entrance gate
   D. let the patrons deposit admission fees in a box at the bathhouse entrance gate

2. If an operator of a four-wheel drive beach buggy leaves the sand portion of a beach and neglects to disengage his forward gears when he starts to drive over area streets to the dump or drop area, he will   2.____

   A. cause his transmission to lose linkage
   B. excessively wear his emergency brake
   C. jam up his front differential
   D. seriously damage the springs of the vehicle

3. Inventories and replacement of material, supplies, and equipment required for pre-season preparation of beaches is normally scheduled to begin immediately after   3.____

   A. April 1st   B. Memorial Day
   C. Labor Day   D. New Year's Day

4. On an Emerson Resuscitator, the cylinder is considered full when the cylinder volume indicator shows AT LEAST _____ lbs. pressure per square inch or more.   4.____

   A. 900   B. 1300   C. 1800   D. 2800

5. The term *deadman,* when used in training courses for lifeguards assigned to oceanfront beaches, refers to   5.____

   A. a rope splicing tool
   B. beach cradles
   C. upland anchorage
   D. a fixed warning sign on a stone jetty

6. The appropriate arm signal for a lifeguard to give from a standing position on his tower to call for delivery of a resuscitator is: 6.____

   A. Pump one arm up and down from an overhead position
   B. Rotary motion in front of chest
   C. Arms extended up -- straight overhead
   D. Arms clasped overhead

7. The standard technique for executing the back pressure - arm lift method of artificial respiration requires the operator to adhere to a cycle consisting of a prescribed series of motions.
   This cycle should be repeated about _____ times per minute.

   A. two   B. four   C. six   D. twelve

8. Assume that an elderly swimmer has collapsed while swimming. His friend, who is with him, states that the victim has a long history of heart failure. The victim is brought to the first aid station showing signs of shock and labored breathing.
   You should take which one of the following actions?

   A. Apply an oxygen mask tightly to the victim's face
   B. Using the resuscitator, turn on the inhalator valve and apply the face mask
   C. Get him dressed and send him to a hospital with his friend
   D. Wrap him in blankets to keep warm and give him a hot beverage

9. The symptoms of heat prostration MOST usually are:

   A. Face pale, pulse weak; perspiration profuse on forehead, face, and hands; faintness and nausea
   B. Face red, hot, and dry; pulse strong and fast, high fever; perhaps nausea
   C. Face purplish; pulse erratic; feet and hands cold
   D. Face pale; respiration rate down to six; patient violent

10. Of the following, the BEST method for controlling algae growth in outdoor swimming pools is to

    A. treat with heavy dosages of chlorine
    B. raise the pH with additional amounts of calcium carbonate
    C. apply standard rates of copper sulphate
    D. lower the pool level and add fresh water from the main

11. To improve the capabilities of swimming pool filters, a jelly-like substance called a *flock* must be deposited on the surface of the filter bed.
    The flock is formed by adding which of the following two chemicals to the water in the treatment tank?

    A. Anhydrous ammonia and sodium dichromate
    B. Aluminum sulphate and sodium carbonate
    C. Orthotolidine and copper sulphate
    D. Iodides and calcium chloride

12. Pool water returning from the center drain of an outdoor swimming pool is called the

    A. confluent   B. effluent   C. influent   D. affluent

13. Backwashing in a conventional water treatment plant is USUALLY performed by the plant operator when the loss of head reaches _____ pounds per square inch.

    A. 3 1/2-4   B. 5 1/2-7   C. 8-10   D. 11-12

14. Most outdoor swimming pool operations have large heating boilers. These boilers have water columns with look-through water gauges, showing the water level in the boiler. The manual on maintenance and operation of heating plants and auxiliary equipment specifies that, while the boiler is in operation, the water column and gauge glass should be blown down 14._____

    A. daily   B. weekly   C. bi-weekly   D. monthly

15. Conventional gun-type oil burners used at park facilities are required to utilize as fuel 15._____

    A. #2 oil   B. #4 oil
    C. #6 oil   D. a kerosene mixture

16. Chlorine residual in municipally operated pools as required by the department of health shall be kept at NOT LESS THAN _____ ppm. 16._____

    A. 0.01   B. 0.25   C. 0.45   D. 1.0

17. Which of the following should be used to test the pH range (alkaline range) of swimming pool water? 17._____

    A. Ultraviolet light   B. Iodides
    C. Orthotolodine   D. Bromthymol blue

18. The filtration rate per square foot for a conventional filter is _____ gallons per square foot. 18._____

    A. 8   B. 6   C. 5   D. 3

19. Chlorine gas in steel cylinders is used as a sterilant in most outdoor swimming pools. If chlorine gas leaks occur from faulty connections, valve packings, etc., the STANDARD procedure for locating the leaks promptly is to use 19._____

    A. a lighted sulphur taper
    B. a soapy mixture
    C. acetone, applied with a camel hair brush
    D. concentrated ammonia

20. The MOST desirable time to apply lime to fairways on a golf course that is high in the acid range is 20._____

    A. during the rainy season   B. after a long, dry spell
    C. in the fall or spring   D. in late January

21. A bag of commercial fertilizer with a 10-6-4 classification on the printed face of the bag contains which of the following combination of chemicals by weight? 21._____

    A. 10% phosphoric acid, 6% nitrogen, and 4% potash
    B. 10% potash, 6% phosphoric acid, and 4% nitrogen
    C. 10% nitrogen, 6% phosphoric acid, and 4% potash
    D. 10% potash, 6% nitrogen, and 4% phosphoric acid

22. The turf on a tee with 15,000 square feet is badly worn because of traffic density and must be completely rehabilitated. You have completed the step requiring the application of a soil sterilant, and you are ready to apply nitrogen to the soil at a rate of two pounds of available nitrogen per thousand square feet.
How many 100 pound bags of 10-6-4 fertilizer must be applied to adequately supply the nitrogen requirements?

    A. 10   B. 8   C. 5   D. 3

22.____

23. According to regulations relating to lawn-making, which of the following pH ratings of fertilizer is desirable?

    A. 4.5 to 5.0   B. 5.5 to 6.0
    C. 6.5 to 7.0   D. 7.5 to 8.0

23.____

24. To facilitate photosynthesis for normal growth, grass should be mowed often enough so that clippings are

    A. equal to mowing height
    B. shorter than mowing height
    C. longer than mowing height
    D. two inches long

24.____

25. Of the following, the MOST suitable grass seed mixture for a play field is one containing Kentucky bluegrass and

    A. colonial bent   B. Bermuda grass
    C. zoysia   D. creeping red fescue

25.____

26. Red fescue is USUALLY added to a seed mixture because of its

    A. drought resistance   B. fast germination
    C. slow germination   D. coarse texture

26.____

27. The four basic procedures generally considered as constituting the minimum maintenance for turf are: (1) selection of adapted grasses; (2) fertilization; (3) watering; and (4)

    A. aerification   B. mowing
    C. plugging   D. rolling

27.____

28. The BEST method for improving the soil structure of a heavily compacted playfield is to apply organic top-dressing first and then proceed with

    A. pesticide application   B. mowing and watering
    C. fertilization   D. aerification

28.____

29. A fairway should be maintained so that its width averages _____ to _____ feet.

    A. 60; 110   B. 120; 210   C. 220; 260   D. 270; 310

29.____

30. A good supplemental program to aid the grass that is already growing and to establish new grass in the thin, worn-out areas of an athletic field is

    A. overseeding   B. rolling
    C. plugging   D. watering

30.____

KEY (CORRECT ANSWERS)

1.	A	11.	B	21.	C
2.	C	12.	B	22.	D
3.	C	13.	B	23.	C
4.	C	14.	A	24.	B
5.	C	15.	A	25.	D
6.	C	16.	D	26.	A
7.	D	17.	D	27.	B
8.	B	18.	D	28.	D
9.	A	19.	D	29.	B
10.	C	20.	C	30.	A

TEST 2

DIRECTIONS: Each question or incomplete statement is followed by several suggested answers or completions. Select the one that BEST answers the question or completes the statement. *PRINT THE LETTER OF THE CORRECT ANSWER IN THE SPACE AT THE RIGHT.*

1. Traps are customarily surfaced with a layer of sand about _____ inches deep.　　1._____
   A. 6　　　B. 12　　　C. 18　　　D. 24

2. A GOOD medium sandy loam for a putting green should contain _____ organic content.　　2._____
   A. 5-10%　　B. 10-15%　　C. 20-30%　　D. 30-50%

3. In the maintenance of a putting green, the LEAST necessary piece of equipment is　　3._____
   A. putting green mower　　B. power sprayer
   C. aerator　　D. fertilizer spreader

4. The BEST way to maintain a green so that it holds a pitched ball is by　　4._____
   A. overwatering　　B. good soil structure
   C. underwatering　　D. high mowing

5. The surface soil on a green should be a medium sandy loam placed _____ to _____ inches deep.　　5._____
   A. 2; 4　　B. 4; 6　　C. 8; 10　　D. 12; 18

6. The BEST turf fertilizers today contain about　　6._____
   A. 85% slow-release phosphorus
   B. 16% fast-release nitrogen
   C. 50% slow-release nitrogen
   D. 20% phosphorus

7. Since golf course grasses are heavy users of phosphorus, potassium, magnesium, and calcium, the BEST pH range for turf, where maximum quantities of these chemicals are available, is　　7._____
   A. 4.2 to 4.8　　B. 5.0 to 5.8
   C. 6.0 to 7.0　　D. 7.2 to 8.2

8. Damage on golf greens and other turf areas caused by the *Fusarium nivale* fungus (snow mold) can BEST be prevented or adequately checked by treatment with　　8._____
   A. ammonium methyl arsenates
   B. aluminum sulphate
   C. hydrated lime
   D. cadminates

9. To prevent snow mold, treatment should GENERALLY start　　9._____
   A. in early spring　　B. after a heavy rain
   C. in late winter　　D. after a heavy snow

10. Chlordane is used in turf management to

    A. eradicate goose grass
    B. control brown patch
    C. grub-proof soil
    D. stimulate root growth

11. Artificial rinks have refrigerants to cool the brine which is constantly circulated through the wrought-iron pipes imbedded in the floor of the rink.
    The brine can be chilled to below zero degrees Fahrenheit because it contains a chemical salt known as

    A. sodium chloride
    B. calcium chloride
    C. calcium carbonate
    D. ammonium chloride

12. The MINIMUM ice thickness generally considered safe for ice skating on a lake or pond whose depth does not exceed 3 feet is _____ inches.

    A. 2   B. 3   C. 5   D. 6

13. In the operation of an ice skating rink, prior to starting the process of ice building, the slab surface should be painted with _____ paint.

    A. white water
    B. white epoxy
    C. blue water
    D. blue epoxy

14. Crowd control in an ice skating rink includes all phases of the patrons' activities from admissions line-up to the time the patrons leave the rink.
    According to regulations, during special sessions, guards should

    A. skate in a clockwise direction
    B. skate in a counterclockwise direction
    C. be positioned on the ice near the entrances
    D. be positioned off the ice near the entrances

15. When a rink slab has been chilled below freezing temperature, ice can be built to the desired thickness by spraying a fine layer of water onto the slab with a

    A. Toro sprayer
    B. Skinner sprinkler
    C. Rainboni
    D. Zamboni

16. The following is a description of the cooling system of a skating rink: The refrigerant (ammonia or freon) absorbs the heat from the circulating brine which, in turn, lowers the temperature of the skating slab; when the brine is returned to the chiller after leaving the rink floor with absorbed heat, the compressor pumps the refrigerant gases to the condenser.
    The condenser does which of the following?
    It

    A. cools the refrigerant gas to a liquid and returns it to the chiller
    B. heats up the refrigerant gas
    C. transforms the gas into ice crystals
    D. cools the circulating water within the condenser

17. At indoor rinks where atmospheric temperatures remain stable and are not affected by outdoor weather conditions, brine should be circulated at a temperature of APPROXIMATELY _____ degrees Fahrenheit.

    A. 7   B. 10   C. 15   D. 25

18. Conditioning ice surfaces on outdoor rinks in early fall or late spring is BEST accomplished

    A. after each session
    B. after the sun sets
    C. at 8 A.M.
    D. at 12 noon

19. The standard of thickness for safe skating on lakes and ponds with water depths over three feet is _____ inches.

    A. two
    B. three
    C. five
    D. seven

20. Assume that a heavy snowstorm has reached the area at the start of the evening session of outdoor rink operations. The one of the following actions that should be taken is to

    A. send all the skaters home, telling them the rink is closed
    B. let them skate until the snow is too deep to move
    C. cone off one-half of the rink at a time for snow removal operations
    D. give snow shovels to as many skaters as possible and put them to work clearing the rink

21. Of the following trees, the one which is NOT recommended for street tree planting is

    A. London plane
    B. Gingko
    C. Yellow Pine
    D. Pin Oak

22. Before useful measures can be applied to control a tree disease epidemic in a park, it is FIRST necessary to

    A. obtain an appropriation for spraying
    B. have a correct diagnosis made of the disease
    C. make an inventory of the diseased trees
    D. wait until winter when the trees are dormant

23. Of the following trees, the one which is generally MOST often recommended for sandy soils is

    A. American elm
    B. Japanese maple
    C. Chinese poplar
    D. Japanese black pine

24. About 75 percent of all tree diseases, including all mildews, rusts, anthracnoses, and sooty molds, are caused by

    A. fungi
    B. viruses
    C. nematodes
    D. bacteria

25. Tree crews should be instructed to ALWAYS

    A. trim the leader of a tree to improve its vitality
    B. prune trees by removing at least 50% of the crowns
    C. remove all injured and diseased wood
    D. fertilize a tree before pruning it

26. Three techniques that you can use to evaluate maintenance activities and determine whether they can be done better are work simplification, work measurement, and

    A. establishment of work performance standards
    B. use of labor saving devices
    C. increased supervision
    D. computerization

27. Staffing is BEST indicated by which of the following activities?

    A. Selection and training of personnel and maintaining favorable conditions of work
    B. Structuring an organization for unity of command, span of control, and lines of authority
    C. Writing task lists for the different titles working at a facility
    D. Working out in broad outline the things that need to be done and the methods for doing them to accomplish the mission of the agency

28. Generally, the MOST practical way to ascertain most readily the number of man-hours it takes to do a job is by

    A. referring to a management analysis handbook
    B. making a detailed analysis of the job
    C. asking the operator performing the job
    D. reviewing job specifications

29. Any violation of the rules or regulations for the government and protection of public parks and property shall be punishable by NOT MORE THAN _____ imprisonment or by a fine of not more than _____ dollars, or by both.

    A. thirty days'; fifty
    B. sixty days'; one hundred
    C. ninety days'; two hundred fifty
    D. one year's; five hundred

30. One workman can hand-rake leaves at the rate of approximately 1,000 square feet in 20 minutes.
    How many men would you assign to a crew to hand rake a grove of trees covering 40,000 square feet in order to accomplish the job within three hours?

    A. 3   B. 30   C. 50   D. 5

KEY (CORRECT ANSWERS)

1.	A	11.	B	21.	C
2.	C	12.	B	22.	B
3.	B	13.	A	23.	D
4.	B	14.	D	24.	A
5.	C	15.	D	25.	C
6.	C	16.	A	26.	A
7.	C	17.	C	27.	A
8.	D	18.	A	28.	C
9.	A	19.	C	29.	A
10.	C	20.	C	30.	D

EXAMINATION SECTION
TEST 1

DIRECTIONS: Each question or incomplete statement is followed by several suggested answers or completions. Select the one that BEST answers the question or completes the statement. *PRINT THE LETTER OF THE CORRECT ANSWER IN THE SPACE AT THE RIGHT.*

1. Assume that a park employee from another district asks you about possible transfers exchanging him and an employee in your district. The two have already discussed it and would like to change.
   For you to DENY such a request is

   A. *advisable;* employees should learn to adjust to their assignments and no one should expect preferential treatment
   B. *inadvisable;* denial may lower work quality and morale when unusual circumstances may be the reason for desiring a change
   C. *inadvisable;* employee requests for transfers always improve work performance of an entire crew
   D. *advisable;* such transfers are never effective and always seem to begin an endless cycle of transfers

   1.____

2. An employee, whom you have reprimanded for low level performance, as begun to work at a level above average.
   For you to PRAISE the employee at least once weekly is a

   A. *good* practice, mainly because the employee will always produce at a higher rate if he know his work is appreciated
   B. *poor* practice, mainly because praise should only be given for an unusually high level of performance
   C. *good* practice, mainly because lack of praise probably caused his low level of performance
   D. *poor* practice, mainly because too much praise seems to lack sincerity

   2.____

3. A laborer reports to you that the park foreman, to whom he is responsible, drinks beer and wine on the job. He states that the foreman's orders are unclear, that he treats his subordinates in an inhumane manner, and he sleeps on the job frequently
   Of the following, the MOST proper action for you to take in this situation is to

   A. tell the employee that you see the foreman every day and he is never intoxicated
   B. ask the employee to keep a secret record of such occurrences and report to you at the end of the month
   C. approach this foreman, along with the laborer who made the complaint, inform him of the allegation, and allow the two to debate the issues
   D. observe this foreman more frequently to discover if the allegation is true and what remedial action need be taken

   3.____

4. You have given a special assignment to an emergency roving work crew to report to a bridge across the horse trail to do some repair work. Of the following, such an order is generally

   4.____

A. *good;* the work order permits the general park supervisor to determine exactly the effectiveness of the roving crew
B. *poor;* the work order tells the crew nothing about the nature, equipment, or manpower needed for the repair
C. *good;* roving crews only need to be told where to go and no further details are necessary
D. *poor;* the general park supervisor should not have to tell the roving crew about a repair, since they should know about it first

5. It is one of your responsibilities to schedule the work hours of all the parks employees in your district.
Of the following, for you to discuss a schedule with your subordinate foremen informally before making it final is generally

   A. *undesirable,* since scheduling is your responsibility and you must not let others influence you in carrying it out
   B. *desirable,* since your subordinates are more likely to accept the schedule if they have had some part in its construction
   C. *undesirable,* since too many conflicting ideas will be received which you cannot resolve
   D. *desirable,* since the blame for any errors in the schedule can be spread among several people

6. A supervisor often gives directives in the form of suggestions rather than as formal orders.
This practice is generally

   A. *desirable,* since a series of formal orders may produce resistance from subordinates
   B. *undesirable,* since suggestions would show indecisiveness
   C. *desirable,* since a supervisor should always act in a friendly manner
   D. *undesirable,* since suggestions would not have to be taken seriously

7. Of the following, the BEST statement about the *grapevine* as a form of communication is that it is

   A. *always destructive* of organization since it only carries gossip and false information
   B. *always useful* because it usually provides more accurate information than formal channels of communication
   C. *often useful* because it provides a channel of communication for information which formal lines of communication cannot suitably carry
   D. *never destructive* of organization since it is only used for harmless, idle gossip

8. The manner in which a supervisor directs his workers usually influences the amount of work which the workers do.
Of the following, workers are MOST likely to produce more work under a supervisor who assigns a job,

   A. instructs in detail how the job is to be done, and closely watches that the job is performed in that way
   B. and leaves it to the workers to figure out how the job is to be done, and checks up only when the job is finished

C. instructs in detail how the job is to be done, and checks the work only when the job is finished
D. leaves the workers to perform it as he has trained them to, and checks occasionally to see that the job is being performed adequately

9. An essential piece of equipment has developed a serious mechanical problem. It can be operated in a limited manner, but will eventually have to go to the district shop for a few weeks for major repairs. Before deciding whether you will have the machine repaired at once or use it as it is for a while, you wish to confer with your foremen. Two of your foremen, however, are new and inexperienced.
Of the following, the BEST statement about including them in the meeting is that such action is generally

    A. *desirable,* since such a meeting will give the men a change from their ordinary work
    B. *undesirable,* since these inexperienced men can contribute nothing and would be just wasting time
    C. *desirable,* since such a meeting with experienced men provides these inexperienced men with an opportunity to learn
    D. *undesirable,* since any ideas offered by these inexperienced men can only confuse the meeting

10. The maintenance of good employee morale is important to high production.
The existence of legitimate grievance channels through which an employee may effectively express dissatisfaction nornally tends, in the long run, to _____ the number of grievances.

    A. *raise* morale while *diminishing*
    B. *lower* morale while *increasing*
    C. *have no effect* on morale or
    D. *raise* morale while *increasing*

11. While making your rounds in the district, you find that one of your men is making a mistake which is clearly due to negligence on his part.
Of the following, your BEST course of action normally is to

    A. reprimand the man at once, loudly, so that other employees in the area will know that you will not tolerate such mistakes
    B. talk to the man privately, letting him know in strong terms that you are personally very angry with him for such performance since it reflects on your superiors' view of you
    C. reprimand the man, then, for several days after, remind him that you are checking his performance so that he will not repeat his negligence
    D. use the situation to train the employee in proper procedure and point out to him the bad effects of negligent work

12. A laborer with an otherwise good work history often comes in late. You ask him why, and he answers, *I just can't get up in the morning. Frankly, I've just lost interest in the job; when I do get up, I've got to rush like crazy to get here.*
Which of the following responses from you would MOST likely lead to a constructive solution of the problem?

A. You don't know what an alarm clock is?
B. Are you having problems with your family?
C. Why have you lost interest in the job?
D. Well, that's no reason for coming in late.

13. A worker over 50 will generally be better than a worker under 25 in all of the following areas EXCEPT

    A. frequency of absences
    B. length of sick-leave absences
    C. safety record
    D. number of grievances

14. Of the following, the advantage for a supervisor in delegating his authority is that such delegation normally provides him with a means to

    A. devote his own time to the more important aspects of a job and assign the less important aspects to his subordinates
    B. keep close personal control over all details in his district
    C. restrict a subordinate's freedom to make wrong decisions
    D. earn his subordinates' respect by working alongside them at the same job

15. In preparing general assignments and work schedules of a group of employees, a supervisor can generally expect the BEST results by making assignments according to which one of the following?

    A. A method which always places workers with similar skills together
    B. A method which takes into account the personalities of the group members
    C. Group preference, which will usually lead to high quality output
    D. A method which does not involve personality factors

16. Workers separated by great distances from the source of authority at the top of the organization have difficulty in *communicating upward.*
    Upward communication MOST NEARLY means

    A. directives that originate with top officials
    B. messages relayed from lower levels to management
    C. communication among workers
    D. a worker's ability to understand formally written orders

17. An angry public works employee tells you about a vending machine concessionaire who has thrown his litter onto the area recently cleaned by the employee. Upon investigation, you discover that the wastebaskets provided for the concessionaire, for which the worker is responsible, are filled to capacity.
    Of the following, the BEST course for you to take in this situation is to

    A. tell the employee that his failure to perform his work is the cause of the trouble; he must improve immediately or be fired
    B. call attention to the employee's poor work record and tell him that he has caused you personal embarrassment
    C. console the employee, tell him that the vendor or another employee is at fault
    D. tell the employee that he should be sure the baskets are properly emptied and if he performs his work correctly, such problems will be eliminated

18. The efficiency of an employee depends in part on the type and quality of training he receives.
Of the following, the BEST method for you to use to train new laborers during a period when personnel is short is to train them

    A. only for the immediate job operation
    B. for more than one operation only if they had prior experience
    C. on a continuous basis so that immediate and long-range job operations are considered
    D. by giving all the details of the job operation during the first training session

18.____

19. A park foreman has indicated to you that a major steel connector on a basketball court in the district needs to be replaced. You then later discover that the extent of the damage on the court requires the removal of the damaged connector immediately.
Of the following, the BEST way to have the connector replaced is for you to report the situation first to the

    A. roving work crew who is directly responsible for all emergencies
    B. regular work crew who is directly responsible for the area
    C. mechanical shop who will replace the connector
    D. senior supervisor of park operations who is directly responsible for property damage

19.____

20. Assume that you were told of a minor incident involving one of the workers and a teen-age boy in the park. The following day, you overhear the true details of the incident which were much more serious than those which you were told.
Why is it that information originating at the lowest level of an organization often reaches higher levels in a completely different form?

    A. Workers at the lowest levels in an organization usually enjoy deceiving their superiors.
    B. Workers often feel that supervisors are their enemy and, therefore, they prefer to keep any information about themselves within their own ranks.
    C. Information starting at the lower levels tends to be stripped of details which might anger or upset the immediate supervisor.
    D. Most supervisors are too busy to be hindered by disciplinary reports about their workers.

20.____

21. While he is preparing for a rock concert expected to draw a capacity crowd, an employee scheduled to assist with the affair is injured. From past experience, you know that Bill is the best replacement for the injured employee.
Of the following, the MOST appropriate action for you to take is to

    A. approach Bill as you would any friend, pointing out your faith in him
    B. tell Bill that you know that someone else is available, but that he is so fussy that you'd rather have him, since he always knows what to do
    C. give Bill an order stating that he will replace the injured employee
    D. tell Bill what has happened so that he understands why he is being asked to work and make him feel that he has a part in an important decision

21.____

22. Following a two-month period of regular inspection procedures and a number of discussions with the foreman and individual laborers about proper maintenance procedures, you still receive complaints from patrons about substandard maintenance of the area adjacent to a swimming pool in your district.
The one of the following which is the MOST appropriate action for you to take is to

    A. hold private sessions with each laborer to find out how to correct the situation
    B. hold a group conference to express your dissatisfaction in clear terms and to give the work crew a chance to present their side of the issue
    C. complain to your superiors to get help concerning the best method of improvement
    D. hold a group conference, calling only upon members of the crew who have performed satisfactorily for improvement ideas

23. Assume that you want to train a new park foreman by rotating him to all blotter stops in your district so he will receive on-the-job training from experienced park foremen. You also plan to hold daily sessions with the new foreman.
Of the following, the MOST correct statement about this procedure is that it is generally

    A. *undesirable;* the new foreman would not know what to do with so many people directing him
    B. *desirable;* a person in the same job position as the new employee would always be helpful
    C. *desirable;* the new foreman would receive varied and needed experience along with supervisory attention
    D. *undesirable;* a person in the same job position always resents new persons and does not properly train them

24. An employee complains to you about what he feels is the overbearing conduct of the park foreman who is his superior.
Of the following, the MOST immediate action that you should generally take is to

    A. reprimand the foreman immediately and demand that he adhere to a more democratic method of supervision
    B. investigate the situation since an employee usually does not find it easy to complain about his superior
    C. dismiss the allegation since most employees enjoy creating problems for others, especially for their superiors
    D. defend the foreman, reminding the employee that the foreman has the proper knowledge and experience to handle his position efficiently

25. During the past three weeks, Frank Parker, usually an efficient employee, has developed an unusual attitude and frequently *pops off* in the presence of other workers. His work performance has fallen below the accepted standard and his attitude has lowered the morale of his work team.
Of the following, the BEST action for you to take is to

    A. reprimand Frank by reminding him that neither his attitude nor his poor work will be tolerated
    B. call Frank in for a conference to discuss his work performance
    C. ignore Frank's behavior, since he has performed well in the past
    D. transfer Frank to other work locations at set intervals, to keep his morale and work standards up

KEY (CORRECT ANSWERS)

1. B
2. D
3. D
4. B
5. B

6. A
7. C
8. D
9. C
10. A

11. D
12. C
13. B
14. A
15. B

16. B
17. D
18. C
19. C
20. C

21. D
22. B
23. C
24. B
25. B

TEST 2

DIRECTIONS: Each question or incomplete statement is followed by several suggested answers or completions. Select the one that BEST answers the question or completes the statement. *PRINT THE LETTER OF THE CORRECT ANSWER IN THE SPACE AT THE RIGHT.*

1. Which of the following is the MOST likely action a supervisor should take to help establish an effective working relationship with his departmental superiors?

    A. Delay the implementation of new procedures received from superiors in order to evaluate their appropriateness
    B. Skip the chain of command whenever he feels that it is to his advantage
    C. Keep supervisors informed of problems in his area and the steps taken to correct them
    D. Don't take up superiors' time by discussing anticipated problems but wait until the difficulties occur

2. Of the following, the action a supervisor could take which would generally be MOST conducive to the establishment of an effective working relationship with employees includes

    A. maintaining impersonal relationships to prevent development of biased actions
    B. treating all employees equally without adjusting for individual differences
    C. continuous observation of employees on the job with insistence on constant improvement
    D. careful planning and scheduling of work for your employees

3. Which of the following procedures is the LEAST likely to establish effective working relationships between employees and supervisors?

    A. Encouraging *two-way* communication with employees
    B. Periodic discussion with employees regarding their job performance
    C. Ignoring employees' gripes concerning job difficulties
    D. Avoiding personal prejudices in dealing with employees

4. Criticism can be used as a tool to point out the weak areas of a subordinate's work performance.
   Of the following, the BEST action for a supervisor to take so that his criticism will be accepted is to

    A. focus his criticism on the act instead of on the person
    B. exaggerate the errors in order to motivate the employee to do better
    C. pass judgment quickly and privately, without investigating the circumstances of the error
    D. generalize the criticism and not specifically point out the errors in performance

5. Assume that it has come to your attention that two of your subordinates have shouted at each other and have almost engaged in a fist fight; luckily, they were separated by some of the other employees.
   Of the following, your BEST immediate course of action would generally be to

A. reprimand the senior of the two subordinates, since he should have known better
B. hear the story from both employees and any witnesses and then take needed disciplinary action
C. ignore the matter, since nobody was physically hurt
D. immediately suspend and fine both employees pending a departmental hearing

6. You have been delegating some of your authority to one of your subordinates because of his leadership potential.
Which of the following actions is LEAST conducive to the growth and development of this individual for a supervisory position?

    A. Use praise only when it will be effective
    B. Give very detailed instructions and supervise the employee closely to be sure that the instructions are followed precisely
    C. Let the subordinate proceed with his planned course of action even if mistakes, within a permissible range, are made
    D. Intervene on behalf of the subordinate whenever an assignment becomes difficult for him

7. A rumor has been spreading in your department concerning the possibility of layoffs due to decreased revenues.
As a supervisor, you should generally

    A. deny the rumor, whether it is true or false, in order to keep morale from declining
    B. inform the men to the best of your knowledge about this situation and keep them advised of any new information
    C. tell the men to forget about the rumor and concentrate on increasing their productivity
    D. ignore the rumor, since it is not authorized information

8. Within an organization, every supervisor should know to whom he reports and who reports to him.
The one of the following which is achieved by use of such structured relationships is

    A. unity of command   B. confidentiality
    C. esprit de corps   D. promotion opportunities

9. While observing a summer aide perform his duties, you notice that he is using many useless motions in completing a task.
In order to improve the productivity of the aid, you generally can BEST use this opportunity to

    A. reprimand the aide for his inefficient performance
    B. point out the aide's inefficiency and compare this performance to other mistakes he has committed, in order to motivate him
    C. provide training for the aide at this time in order to increase his future work productivity
    D. let the aide learn by doing

10. While spot-checking the activities of summer park aides, you notice a few of them engaging in *horseplay*.
Of the following, the MOST appropriate action for you to take would be to

A. tell the summer park aides to immediately stop the *horseplay* and continue with their work
B. ignore their actions if their work is progressing satisfactorily; after all, *horseplay* is normal among youthful employees
C. reprimand the aides by telling them to go home for the day
D. report this incident to the aides' immediate supervisor when you see him

11. Of the following, the action of a supervisor that would be LEAST likely to give the general public a favorable impression of the parks department would be to

    A. provide information concerning the department's interest in community affairs
    B. acquaint friends and others with departmental activities that provide a favorable view of the department
    C. speak unfavorably of the working conditions established by the department
    D. participate in and support civic and community activities

12. Assume that it has come to your attention that small amounts of minor park supplies and materials have been disappearing.
    Of the following, the BEST statement about ignoring this situation is that to do so is

    A. *desirable;* since no large thefts have occurred, it would be better to forget about the little items
    B. *desirable;* since the work is being done, there is no reason to upset the workers
    C. *undesirable;* the park may have to close due to the thefts of supplies
    D. *undesirable;* you would be condoning such acts unless you take immediate steps to curtail these occurrences

13. Several members of a work crew have approached you with the idea of rotating men on job assignments such as raking leaves, picking up paper, and making minor repairs on the tennis courts.
    Of the following, your BEST answer would be:

    A. I'm sorry, but such a change would make it impossible to keep track of who does what
    B. If you all agree to the change, let's try it
    C. I'm not sure if that is allowed. I'll send in some papers and notify you in a couple of weeks
    D. The work is getting done now. Leave things as they are

14. Which of the following is generally the MOST effective way for you to communicate information to the workers?

    A. Face-to-face communication
    B. A notice on the bulletin board
    C. The telephone
    D. A messenger with a memo

15. While walking through the playground, you find one of the workers sitting on a park bench. He has done an excellent job of cleaning the area; and when you approach him, he says that he is *just taking a short break.*
    Of the following, the MOST acceptable course of action for you to take in this situation is to

A. tell him there is plenty of work still to be done
B. tell him to save his rests for lunch breaks
C. pretend that you don't see him
D. tell him that he is entitled to a quick break because he has done a good job, but to make it a small break

16. Assume that you have found out that one of the workers usually drinks alcohol heavily on his lunch hour.
Of the following, the BEST course of action for you to take in such a situation is to

    A. try to isolate him so that he will not influence the other workers
    B. call his wife and ask her for her help
    C. tactfully suggest that he seek professional help
    D. try to find the cause of his problem and help him solve it

16.____

17. Penetrating oil is OFTEN used for

    A. cutting pipe
    B. loosening rusted bolts
    C. clearing clogged pipes
    D. lubricating electric appliances

17.____

18. Sweating or condensation of moisture on the outside of a pipe is MOST likely to occur on _____ pipes.

    A. hot water   B. steam
    C. cold water   D. compressed air

18.____

19. Turpentine may be used as a thinner for

    A. shellac   B. latex paints
    C. calcimine   D. oil paints

19.____

20. Creosote is COMMONLY used to

    A. preserve wood from rot
    B. fireproof wood structures
    C. change the color of wood
    D. hasten the seasoning of wood

20.____

21. The MOST commonly used welding torches are fed by two tanks of gas. One of these tanks holds acetylene and the other holds

    A. carbon dioxide   B. hydrogen
    C. nitrogen   D. oxygen

21.____

22. When 8-32 is used to designate a screw, the figures represent, respectively,

    A. threads/inch and diameter
    B. length and diameter
    C. diameter and length
    D. diameter and threads/inch

22.____

23. Galvanized pipe has a finish coating of

    A. lead   B. zinc   C. copper   D. nickel

23.____

24. It is not considered good practice to paint portable wooden ladders. Of the following, the MOST logical reason for this is that the

    A. painted rungs would become slippery when wet
    B. paint might rub off on a supporting wall
    C. paint might hide serious defects
    D. paint would quickly wear off

25. The type of fastener MOST commonly used when bolting to concrete uses a(n)

    A. expansion shield
    B. U-bolt
    C. toggle bolt
    D. turnbuckle

KEY (CORRECT ANSWERS)

1.	C	11.	C
2.	D	12.	D
3.	C	13.	B
4.	A	14.	A
5.	B	15.	D
6.	B	16.	C
7.	B	17.	B
8.	A	18.	C
9.	C	19.	D
10.	A	20.	A

21. D
22. D
23. B
24. C
25. A

EDUCATING AND INTERACTING WITH THE PUBLIC

These questions test for knowledge of techniques used to interact effectively with individual citizens and/or community groups, to educate or inform them about topics of concern, to publicize or clarify agency programs or policies, to negotiate conflicts or resolve complaints, and to represent one's agency or program in a manner in keeping with good public relations practices. Questions may also cover interacting with others in cooperative efforts of public outreach or service. There will be 15 questions in this subject area on the written test.

TEST TASK:
You will be presented with a variety of situations in which you must apply knowledge of how best to interact with other people.

SAMPLE QUESTION:
A person approaches you expressing anger about a recent action by your department. Which one of the following should be your first response to this person?

A. Interrupt to say you cannot discuss the situation until he calms down.
B. Say you are sorry that he has been negatively affected by your department's action.
C. Listen and express understanding that he has been upset by your department's action.
D. Give him an explanation of the reasons for your department's action.

The correct answer to this sample question is choice C

C. SOLUTION:

Choice A *is not correct.* It would be inappropriate to interrupt. In addition, saying that you cannot discuss the situation until the person calms down will likely aggravate him further.

Choice B *is not correct.* Apologizing for your department's action implies that the action was improper.

Choice C is the correct answer to this question. By listening and expressing understanding that your department's action has upset him, you demonstrate that you have heard and understand his feelings and point of view.

Choice D *is not correct.* While an explanation of the reasons for the action may be appropriate at a later time, at this moment the person is angry and would not be receptive to such an explanation.

EXAMINATION SECTION
TEST 1

DIRECTIONS: Each question or incomplete statement is followed by several suggested answers or completions. Select the one that BEST answers the question or completes the statement. *PRINT THE LETTER OF THE CORRECT ANSWER IN THE SPACE AT THE RIGHT.*

1. When conducting a needs assessment for the purpose of education planning, an agency's FIRST step is to identify or provide
    A. a profile of population characteristics
    B. barriers to participation
    C. existing resources
    D. profiles of competing resources

    1._____

2. Research has demonstrated that of the following, the MOST effective medium for communicating with external publics is(are)
    A. video news releases
    B. television
    C. radio
    D. newspapers

    2._____

3. Basic ideas behind the effort to influence the attitudes and behaviors of a constituency include each of the following EXCEPT the idea that
    A. words, rather than actions or events, are most likely to motivate
    B. demands for action are a usual response
    C. self-interest usually figures heavily into public involvement
    D. the reliability of change programs is difficult to assess

    3._____

4. An agency representative is trying to craft a pithy message to constituents in order to encourage the use of agency program resources.
    Choosing an audience for such messages is easiest when the message
    A. is project- or behavior-based
    B. is combined with other messages
    C. is abstract
    D. has a broad appeal

    4._____

5. Of the following factors, the MOST important to the success of an agency's external education or communication programs is the
    A. amount of resources used to implement them
    B. public's prior experiences with the agency
    C. real value of the program to the public
    D. commitment of the internal audience

    5._____

6. A representative for a state agency is being interviewed by a reporter from a local news network. The representative is being asked to defend a program that is extremely unpopular in certain parts of the municipality.
    When a constituency is known to be opposed to a position, the MOST useful communication strategy is to present

    6._____

A. only the arguments that are consistent with constituents' views
B. only the agency's side of the issue
C. both sides of the argument as clearly as possible
D. both sides of the argument, omitting key information about the opposing position

7. The MOST significant barriers to effective agency community relations include
   I. widespread distrust of communication strategies
   II. the media's "watchdog" stance
   III. public apathy
   IV. statutory opposition

   The CORRECT answer is:
   A. I only   B. I and II   C. II and III   D. III and IV

8. In conducting an education program, many agencies use workshops and seminars in a classroom setting.
   Advantages of classroom-style teaching over other means of educating the public include each of the following, EXCEPT
   A. enabling an instructor to verify learning through testing and interaction with the target audience
   B. enabling hands-on practice and other participatory learning techniques
   C. ability to reach an unlimited number of participants in a given length of time
   D. ability to convey the latest, most up-to-date information

9. The _____ model of community relations is characterized by an attempt to persuade the public to adopt the agency's point of view.
   A. two-way symmetric   B. two-way asymmetric
   C. public information   D. press agency/publicity

10. Important elements of an internal situation analysis include the
    I. list of agency opponents   II. communication audit
    III. updated organizational almanac IV. stakeholder analysis

    The CORRECT answer is:
    A. I and II   B. I, II, and III   C. II and III   D. I, II, III and IV

11. Government agency information efforts typically involve each of the following objectives, EXCEPT to
    A. implement changes in the policies of government agencies to align with public opinion
    B. communicate the work of agencies
    C. explain agency techniques in a way that invites input from citizens
    D. provide citizen feedback to government administrators

12. Factors that are likely to influence the effectiveness of an educational campaign include the
    I. level of homogeneity among intended participants
    II. number and types of media used
    III. receptivity of the intended participants
    IV. level of specificity in the message or behavior to be taught

    The CORRECT answer is:
    A. I and II   B. I, II, and III   C. II and III   D. I, II, III, and IV

13. An agency representative is writing instructional objectives that will later help to measure the effectiveness of an educational program.
    Which of the following verbs, included in an objective, would be MOST helpful for the purpose of measuring effectiveness?
    A. Know   B. Identify   C. Learn   D. Comprehend

14. A state education agency wants to encourage participation in a program that has just received a boost through new federal legislation. The program is intended to include participants from a wide variety of socioeconomic and other demographic characteristics. The agency wants to launch a broad-based program that will inform virtually every interested party in the state about the program's new circumstances.
    In attempting to deliver this message to such a wide-ranging constituency, the agency's BEST practice would be to
    A. broadcast the same message through as many different media channels as possible
    B. focus on one discrete segment of the public at a time
    C. craft a message whose appeal is as broad as the public itself
    D. let the program's achievements speak for themselves and rely on word-of-mouth

15. Advantages associated with using the World Wide Web as an educational tool include
    I. an appeal to younger generations of the public
    II. visually-oriented, interactive learning
    III. learning that is not confined by space, time, or institutional association
    IV. a variety of methods for verifying use and learning

    The CORRECT answer is:
    A. I only   B. I and II   C. I, II, and III   D. I, II, II, and IV

16. In agencies involved in health care, community relations is a critical function because it
    A. serves as an intermediary between the agency and consumers
    B. generates a clear mission statement for agency goals and priorities
    C. ensures patient privacy while satisfying the media's right to information
    D. helps marketing professionals determine the wants and needs of agency constituents

17. After an extensive campaign to promote its newest program to constituents, an agency learns that most of the audience did not understand the intended message.
MOST likely, the agency has
   A. chosen words that were intended to inform, rather than persuade
   B. not accurately interpreted what the audience really needed to know
   C. overestimated the ability of the audience to receive and process the message
   D. compensated for noise that may have interrupted the message

18. The necessary elements that lead to conviction and motivation in the minds of participants in an educational or information program include each of the following, EXCEPT the _____ of the message.
   A. acceptability
   B. intensity
   C. single-channel appeal
   D. pervasiveness

19. Printed materials are often at the core of educational programs provided by public agencies.
The PRIMARY disadvantage associated with print is that it
   A. does not enable comprehensive treatment of a topic
   B. is generally unreliable in term of assessing results
   C. is often the most expensive medium available
   D. is constrained by time

20. Traditional thinking on public opinion holds that there is about _____ percent of the public who are pivotal to shifting the balance and momentum of opinion—they are concerned about an issue, but not fanatical, and interested enough to pay attention to a reasoned discussion.
   A. 2
   B. 10
   C. 33
   D. 51

21. One of the most useful guidelines for influencing attitude change among people is to
   A. invite the target audience to come to you, rather than approaching them
   B. use moral appeals as the primary approach
   C. use concrete images to enable people to see the results of behaviors or indifference
   D. offer tangible rewards to people for changes in behavior

22. An agency is attempting to evaluate the effectiveness of its educational program. For this purpose, it wants to observe several focus groups discussing the same program.
Which of the following would NOT be a guideline for the use of focus groups?
   A. Focus groups should only include those who have participated in the program.
   B. Be sure to accurately record the discussion.
   C. The same questions should be asked at each focus group meeting.
   D. It is often helpful to have a neutral, non-agency employee facilitate discussions.

5 (#1)

23. Research consistently shows that _____ is the determinant most likely to make a newspaper editor run a news release.
    A. novelty   B. prominence   C. proximity   D. conflict

    23._____

24. Which of the following is NOT one of the major variables to take into account when considering a population-needs assessment?
    A. State of program development   B. Resources available
    C. Demographics   D. Community attitudes

    24._____

25. The FIRST step in any communications audit is to
    A. develop a research instrument
    B. determine how the organization currently communicates
    C. hire a contractor
    D. determine which audience to assess

    25._____

KEY (CORRECT ANSWERS)

1.	A	11.	A
2.	D	12.	D
3.	A	13.	B
4.	A	14.	B
5.	D	15.	C
6.	C	16.	A
7.	D	17.	B
8.	C	18.	C
9.	B	19.	B
10.	C	20.	B

21. C
22. A
23. C
24. C
25. D

TEST 2

DIRECTIONS: Each question or incomplete statement is followed by several suggested answers or completions. Select the one that BEST answers the question or completes the statement. *PRINT THE LETTER OF THE CORRECT ANSWER IN THE SPACE AT THE RIGHT.*

1. A public relations practitioner at an agency has just composed a press release highlighting a program's recent accomplishments and success stories.
   In pitching such releases to print outlets, the practitioner should
   I. e-mail, mail, or send them by messenger
   II. address them to "editor" or "news director"
   III. have an assistant call all media contacts by telephone
   IV. ask reporters or editors how they prefer to receive them

   The CORRECT answer is:
   A. I and II B. I and IV C. II, III, and IV D. III only

   1.____

2. The "output goals" of an educational program are MOST likely to include
   A. specified ratings of services by participants on a standardized scale
   B. observable effects on a given community or clientele
   C. the number of instructional hours provided
   D. the number of participants served

   2.____

3. An agency wants to evaluate satisfaction levels among program participants, and mails out questionnaires to everyone who has been enrolled in the last year.
   The PRIMARY problem associated with this method of evaluative research is that it
   A. poses a significant inconvenience for respondents
   B. is inordinately expensive
   C. does not allow for follow-up or clarification questions
   D. usually involves a low response rate

   3.____

4. A communications audit is an important tool for measuring
   A. the depth of penetration of a particular message or program
   B. the cost of the organization's information campaigns
   C. how key audiences perceive an organization
   D. the commitment of internal stakeholders

   4.____

5. The "ABCs" of written learning objectives include each of the following, EXCEPT
   A. Audience B. Behavior C. Conditions D. Delineation

   5.____

6. When attempting to change the behaviors of constituents, it is important to keep in mind that
   I. most people are skeptical of communications that try to get them to change their behaviors
   II. in most cases, a person selects the media to which he exposes himself
   III. people tend to react defensively to messages or programs that rely on fear as a motivating factor
   IV. programs should aim for the broadest appeal possible in order to include as many participants as possible

   The CORRECT answer is:
   A. I and II   B. I, II and III   C. II and III   D. I, II, III, and IV

7. The "laws" of public opinion include the idea that it is
   A. useful for anticipating emergencies
   B. not sensitive to important events
   C. basically determined by self-interest
   D. sustainable through persistent appeals

8. Which of the following types of evaluations is used to measure public attitudes before and after an information/educational program?
   A. Retrieval study   B. Copy test
   C. Quota sampling   D. Benchmark study

9. The PRIMARY source for internal communications is(are) usually
   A. flow charts   B. meetings
   C. voice mail   D. printed publications

10. An agency representative is putting together informational materials—brochures and a newsletter—outlining changes in one of the state's biggest benefits programs.
    In assembling print materials as a medium for delivering information to the public, the representative should keep in mind each of the following trends:
    I. For various reasons, the reading capabilities of the public are in general decline
    II. Without tables and graphs to help illustrate the changes, it is unlikely that the message will be delivered effectively
    III. Professionals and career-oriented people are highly receptive to information written in the form of a journal article or empirical study
    IV. People tend to be put off by print materials that use itemized and bulleted (●) lists

    The CORRECT answer is:
    A. I and II   B. I, II and III   C. II and III   D. I, II, III, and IV

11. Which of the following steps in a problem-oriented information campaign would typically be implemented FIRST?
    A. Deciding on tactics
    B. Determining a communications strategy
    C. Evaluating the problem's impact
    D. Developing an organizational strategy

12. A common pitfall in conducting an educational program is to
    A. aim it at the wrong target audience
    B. overfund it
    C. leave it in the hands of people who are in the business of education, rather than those with expertise in the business of the organization
    D. ignore the possibility that some other organization is meeting the same educational need for the target audience

13. The key factors that affect the credibility of an agency's educational program include
    A. organization
    B. scope
    C. sophistication
    D. penetration

14. Research on public opinion consistently demonstrates that it is
    A. easy to move people toward a strong opinion on anything, as long as they are approached directly through their emotions
    B. easier to move people away from an opinion they currently hold than to have them form an opinion about something they have not previously cared about
    C. easy to move people toward a strong opinion on anything, as long as the message appeals to their reason and intellect
    D. difficult to move people toward a strong opinion on anything, no matter what the approach

15. In conducting an education program, many agencies use meetings and conferences to educate an audience about the organization and its programs. Advantages associated with this approach include
    I. a captive audience that is known to be interested in the topic
    II. ample opportunities for verifying learning
    III. cost-efficient meeting space
    IV. the ability to provide information on a wider variety of subjects

    The CORRECT answer is:
    A. I and II   B. I, III and IV   C. II and III   D. I, II, III and IV

16. An agency is attempting to evaluate the effectiveness of its educational programs. For this purpose, it wants to observe several focus groups discussing particular programs.
    For this purpose, a focus group should never number more than _____ participants.
    A. 5   B. 10   C. 15   D. 20

17. A _____ speech is written so that several agency members can deliver it to different audiences with only minor variations.
    A. basic   B. printed   C. quota   D. pattern

18. Which of the following statements about public opinion is generally considered to be FALSE?
    A. Opinion is primarily reactive rather than proactive.
    B. People have more opinions about goals than about the means by which to achieve them.
    C. Facts tend to shift opinion in the accepted direction when opinion is not solidly structured.
    D. Public opinion is based more on information than desire.

19. An agency is trying to promote its educational program.
    As a general rule, the agency should NOT assume that
    A. people will only participate if they perceive an individual benefit
    B. promotions need to be aimed at small, discrete groups
    C. if the program is good, the audience will find out about it
    D. a variety of methods, including advertising, special events, and direct mail, should be considered

20. In planning a successful educational program, probably the first and most important question for an agency to ask is:
    A. What will be the content of the program?
    B. Who will be served by the program?
    C. When is the best time to schedule the program?
    D. Why is the program necessary?

21. Media kits are LEAST likely to contain
    A. fact sheets   B. memoranda
    C. photographs with captions D. news releases

22. The use of pamphlets and booklets as media for communication with the public often involves the disadvantage that
    A. the messages contained within them are frequently nonspecific
    B. it is difficult to measure their effectiveness in delivering the message
    C. there are few opportunities for people to refer to them
    D. color reproduction is poor

23. The MOST important prerequisite of a good educational program is an
    A. abundance of resources to implement it
    B. individual staff unit formed for the purpose of program delivery
    C. accurate needs assessment
    D. uneducated constituency

24. After an education program has been delivered, an agency conducts a program evaluation to determine whether its objectives have been met.
General rules about how to conduct such an education program valuation include each of the following, EXCEPT that it
   A. must be done immediately after the program has been implemented
   B. should be simple and easy to use
   C. should be designed so that tabulation of responses can take place quickly and inexpensively
   D. should solicit mostly subjective, open-ended responses if the audience was large

25. Using electronic media such as television as means of educating the public is typically recommended ONLY for agencies that
   I. have a fairly simple message to begin with
   II. want to reach the masses, rather than a targeted audience
   III. have substantial financial resources
   IV. accept that they will not be able to measure the results of the campaign with much precision

   The CORRECT answer is:
   A. I and II   B. I, II and III   C. II and IV   D. I, II, III and IV

KEY (CORRECT ANSWERS)

1.	B	11.	C
2.	C	12.	D
3.	D	13.	A
4.	C	14.	D
5.	D	15.	B
6.	B	16.	B
7.	C	17.	D
8.	D	18.	D
9.	D	19.	C
10.	A	20.	D

21. B
22. B
23. C
24. D
25. D

EXAMINATION SECTION
TEST 1

DIRECTIONS: Each question or incomplete statement is followed by several suggested answers or completions. Select the one that BEST answers the question or completes the statement. *PRINT THE LETTER OF THE CORRECT ANSWER IN THE SPACE AT THE RIGHT.*

1. Although some kinds of instructions are best put in written form, a supervisor can give many instructions verbally.
   In which one of the following situations would verbal instructions be MOST suitable?
   A. Furnishing an employee with the details to be checked in doing a certain job
   B. Instructing an employee on the changes necessary to update the office manual used in your unit
   C. Informing a new employee where different kinds of supplies and equipment that he might need are kept
   D. Presenting an assignment to an employee who will be held accountable for following a series of steps

   1.____

2. You may be asked to evaluate the organization structure of your unit.
   Which one of the following questions would you NOT expect to take up in an evaluation of this kind?
   A. Is there an employee whose personal problems are interfering with his or her work?
   B. Is there an up-to-date job description for each position in this section?
   C. Are related operations and tasks grouped together and regularly assigned together?
   D. Are responsibilities divided as far as possible, and is this division clearly understood by all employees?

   2.____

3. In order to distribute and schedule work fairly and efficiently, a supervisor may wish to make a work distribution study. A simple way of getting the information necessary for such a study is to have everyone for one week keep track of each task doe and the time spent on each.
   Which one of the following situations showing up in such study would MOST clearly call for corrective action?
   A. The newest employee takes longer to do most tasks than do experienced employees.
   B. One difficult operation takes longer to do than most other operations carried out by the section.
   C. A particular employee is very frequently assigned tasks that are not similar and have no relationship to each other.
   D. The most highly skilled employee is often assigned the most difficult jobs.

   3.____

2 (#1)

4. The authority to carry out a job can be delegated to a subordinate, but the supervisor remains responsible for the work of the section as a whole.
As a supervisor, which of the following rules would be the BEST one for you to follow in view of the above statement?
   A. Avoid assigning important tasks to your subordinates, because you will be blamed if anything goes wrong
   B. Be sure each subordinate understands the specific job he has been assigned, and check at intervals to make sure assignments are done properly
   C. Assign several people to every important job so that responsibility will be spread out as much as possible
   D. Have an experienced subordinate check all work done by other employees so that there will be little chance of anything going wrong

4.____

5. The human tendency to resist change is often reflected in higher rates of turnover, absenteeism, and errors whenever an important change is made in an organization. Although psychologists do not fully understand the reasons why people resist change, they believe that the resistance stems from a threat to the individual's security, that it is a form of fear of the unknown.
In light of this statement, which one of the following approaches would probably be MOST effective in preparing employees for a change in procedure in their unit?
   A. Avoid letting employees know anything about the change until the last possible moment
   B. Sympathize with employees who resent the change and let them know you share their doubts and fears
   C. Promise the employees that if the change turns out to be a poor one, you will allow them to suggest a return to the old system
   D. Make sure that employees know the reasons for the change and are aware of the benefits that are expected from it

5.____

6. Each of the following methods of encouraging employee participation in work planning has been used effectively with different kinds and sizes of employee groups.
Which one of the following methods would be MOST suitable for a group of four technically skilled employees?
   A. Discussions between the supervisor and a representative of the group
   B. A suggestion program with semi-annual awards for outstanding suggestions
   C. A group discussion summoned whenever a major problem remains unsolved for more than a month
   D. Day-to-day exchange of information, opinions, and experience

6.____

7. Of the following, the MOST important reason why a supervisor is given the authority to tell subordinates what work they should do, how they should do it, and when it should be done is that usually
   A. most people will not work unless there is someone with authority standing over them

7.____

B. work is accomplished more effectively if the supervisor plans and coordinates it
C. when division of work is left up to subordinates, there is constant arguing, and very little work is accomplished
D. subordinates are not familiar with the tasks to be performed

8. Fatigue is a factor that affects productivity in all work situations. However, a brief rest period will ordinarily serve to restore a person from fatigue.
According to this statement, which one of the following techniques is MOST likely to reduce the impact of fatigue on overall productivity in a unit?
   A. Scheduling several short breaks throughout the day
   B. Allowing employees to go home early
   C. Extending the lunch period an extra half hour
   D. Rotating job assignments every few weeks

9. After giving a new task to an employee, it is a good idea for a supervisor to ask specific questions to make sure that the employee grasps the essentials of the task and sees how it can be carried out. Questions which ask the employee what he thinks or how he feels about an important aspect of the task are particularly effective.
Which one of the following questions is NOT the type of question which would be useful in the foregoing situation?
   A. Do you feel there will be any trouble meeting the 4:30 deadline?
   B. How do you feel about the kind of work we do here?
   C. Do you think that combining those two steps will work all right?
   D. Can you think of any additional equipment you may need for this process?

10. Of the following, the LEAST important reason for having a *continuous* training program is that
    A. employees may forget procedures that they have already learned
    B. employees may develop shortcuts on the job that result in inaccurate work
    C. the job continue to change because of new procedures and equipment
    D. training is one means of measuring effectiveness and productivity on the job

11. In training a new employee, it is usually advisable to break down the job into meaningful parts and have the new employee master one part before going on to the next.
Of the following, the BEST reason for using this technique is to
    A. let the new employee know the reason for what he is doing and thus encourage him to remain in the unit
    B. make the employee aware of the importance of the work and encourage him to work harder
    C. show the employee that the work is easy so that he will be encouraged to work faster
    D. make it more likely that the employee will experience success and will be encouraged to continue learning the job

12. You may occasionally find a serious error in the work of one of your subordinates.
    Of the following, the BEST time to discuss such an error with an employee usually is
    A. immediately after the error is found
    B. after about two weeks, since you will also be able to point out some good things that the employee has accomplished
    C. when you have discovered a pattern of errors on the part of this employee so that he will not be able to dispute your criticism
    D. after the error results in a complaint by your own supervisor

13. For very important announcements to the staff, a supervisor should usually use both written and oral communications. For example, when a new procedure is to be introduced, the supervisor can more easily obtain the group's acceptance by giving his subordinates a rough draft of the new procedure and calling a meeting of all his subordinates.
    The LEAST important benefit of this technique is that it will better enable the supervisor to
    A. explain why the change is necessary
    B. make adjustments in the new procedure to meet valid staff objections
    C. assign someone to carry out the new procedure
    D. answer questions about the new procedure

14. Assume that, while you are interviewing an individual to obtain information, the individual pauses in the middle of an answer.
    The BEST of the following actions for you to take at that time is to
    A. correct any inaccuracies in what he has said
    B. remain silent until he continues
    C. explain your position on the matter being discussed
    D. explain that time is short and that he must complete his story quickly

15. When you are interviewing someone to obtain information, the BEST of the following reasons for you to repeat certain of his exact words is to
    A. assure him that appropriate action will be taken
    B. encourage him to switch to another topic of discussion
    C. assure him that you agree with his point of view
    D. encourage him to elaborate on a point he has made

16. Generally, when writing a letter, the use of precise words and concise sentences is
    A. *good*, because less time will be required to write the letter
    B. *bad*, because it is most likely that the reader will think the letter is unimportant and will not respond favorably
    C. *good*, because it is likely that your desired meaning will be conveyed to the reader
    D. *bad*, because your letter will be too brief to provide adequate information

17. In which of the following cases would it be MOST desirable to have two cards for one individual in a single alphabetic file?
   The individual has
   A. a hyphenated surname
   B. two middle names
   C. a first name with an unusual spelling
   D. a compound first name

18. Of the following, it is MOST appropriate to use a form letter when it is necessary to answer many
   A. requests or inquiries from a single individual
   B. follow-up letters from individuals requesting additional information
   C. request or inquiries about a single subject
   D. complaints from individuals that they have been unable to obtain various types of information

19. Assume that you are asked to make up a budget for your section for the coming year, and you are told that the most important function of the budget is its "control function."
   Of the following, "control" in this context implies MOST NEARLY that
   A. you will probably be asked to justify expenditures in any category when it looks as though these expenditures are departing greatly from the amount budgeted
   B. your section will probably not be allowed to spend more than the budgeted amount in any given category, although it is always permissible to spend less
   C. your section will be required to spend the exact amount budgeted in every category
   D. the budget will be filed in the Office of the Comptroller so that when a year is over the actual expenditures can be compared with the amounts in the budget

20. In writing a report, the practice of taking up the LEAST important points *first* and the most important points *last* is a
   A. *good* technique, since the final points made in a report will make the greatest impression on the reader
   B. *good* technique, since the material is presented in a more logical manner and will lead directly to the conclusions
   C. *poor* technique, since the reader's time is wasted by having to review irrelevant information before finishing the report
   D. *poor* technique, since it may cause the reader to lose interest in the report and arrive at incorrect conclusions about the report

21. Typically, when the technique of "supervision by results" is practiced, higher management sets down, either implicitly or explicitly, certain performance standards or goals that the subordinate is expected to meet. So long as these standards are met, management interferes very little.
   The MOST likely result of the use of this technique is that it will

A. lead to ambiguity in terms of goals
B. be successful only to the extent that close direct supervision is practiced
C. make it possible to evaluate both employee and supervisory effectiveness
D. allow for complete dependence on the subordinate's part

22. When making written evaluations and reviews of the performance of subordinates, it is usually ADVISABLE to
    A. avoid informing the employee of the evaluation if it is critical because it may create hard feelings
    B. avoid informing the employee of the evaluation whether critical or favorable because it is tension-producing
    C. to permit the employee to see the evaluation but not to discuss it with him because the supervisor cannot be certain where the discussion might lead
    D. to discuss the evaluation openly with the employee because it helps the employee understand what is expected of him

23. There are a number of well-known and respected human relations principles that successful supervisors have been using for years in building good relationships with their employees.
    Which of the following does NOT illustrate such a principle?
    A. Give clear and complete instructions
    B. Let each person know how he is getting along
    C. Keep an open-door policy
    D. Make all relationships personal ones

24. Assume that it is necessary for you to give an unpleasant assignment to one of your subordinates. You expect this employee to raise some objections to this assignment.
    The MOST appropriate of the following actions for you to take FIRST is to issue the assignment
    A. *orally*, with the further statement that you will not listen to any complaints
    B. *in writing*, to forestall any complaints by the employee
    C. *orally*, permitting the employee to express his feelings
    D. *in writing*, with a note that any comments should be submitted in writing

25. Suppose you have just announced at a staff meeting with your subordinates that a radical reorganization of work will take place next week. Your subordinates at the meeting appear to be excited, tense, and worried.
    Of the following, the BEST action for you to take at that time is to
    A. schedule private conferences with each subordinate to obtain his reaction to the meeting
    B. close the meeting and tell your subordinates to return immediately to their work assignments
    C. give your subordinates some time to ask questions and discuss your announcement
    D. insist that your subordinates do not discuss your announcement among themselves or with other members of the agency

KEY (CORRECT ANSWERS)

1. C
2. A
3. C
4. B
5. D

6. D
7. B
8. A
9. B
10. D

11. D
12. A
13. C
14. B
15. D

16. C
17. A
18. C
19. A
20. D

21. C
22. D
23. D
24. C
25. C

TEST 2

DIRECTIONS: Each question or incomplete statement is followed by several suggested answers or completions. Select the one that BEST answers the question or completes the statement. *PRINT THE LETTER OF THE CORRECT ANSWER IN THE SPACE AT THE RIGHT.*

1. Of the following, the BEST way for a supervisor to increase employees' interest in their work is to
    A. allow them to make as many decisions as possible
    B. demonstrate to them that he is as technically competent as they
    C. give each employee a difficult assignment
    D. promptly convey to them instructions from higher management

    1.____

2. The one of the following which is LEAST important in maintaining a high level of productivity on the part of employees is the
    A. provision of optimum physical working conditions for employees
    B. strength of employees' aspirations for promotion
    C. anticipated satisfactions which employees hope to derive from their work
    D. employees' interest in their jobs

    2.____

3. Of the following, the MAJOR advantage of group problem-solving, as compared to individual problem-solving, is that groups will more readily
    A. abide by their own decisions
    B. agree with agency management
    C. devise new policies and procedures
    D. reach conclusions sooner

    3.____

4. The group problem-solving conference is a useful supervisory method for getting people to reach solutions to problems.
    Of the following, the reason that groups usually reach more realistic solutions than do individuals is that
    A. individuals, as a rule, take longer than do groups in reaching decisions and are, therefore, more likely to make an error
    B. bringing people together to let them confer impresses participants with the seriousness of problems
    C. groups are generally more concerned with the future in evaluating organizational problems
    D. the erroneous opinions of group members tend to be corrected by the other members

    4.____

5. A competent supervisor should be able to distinguish between human and technical problems.
    Of the following, the MAJOR difference between such problems is that serious human problems, in comparison to ordinary technical problems
    A. are remedied more quickly
    B. involve a lesser need for diagnosis
    C. are more difficult to define
    D. become known through indications which are usually the actual problem

    5.____

6. Of the following, the BEST justification for a public agency establishing an alcoholism program for its employees is that
   A. alcoholism has traditionally been looked upon with a certain amused tolerance by management and thereby ignored as a serious illness
   B. employees with drinking problems have twice as many on-the-job accidents, especially during the early years of the problem
   C. excessive use of alcohol is associated with personality instability hindering informal social relationships among peers and subordinates
   D. the agency's public reputation will suffer despite an employee's drinking problem being a personal matter of little public concern

6._____

7. Assume you are a manager and you find a group of maintenance employees assigned to your project drinking and playing cards for money in an incinerator room after their regular working hours.
   The one of the following actions it would be BEST for you to take is to
   A. suspend all employees immediately if there is no question in your mind as to the validity of the charges
   B. review the personnel records of those involved with the supervisor and make a joint decision on which employees should sustain penalties of loss of annual leave or fines
   C. ask the supervisor to interview each violator and submit written reports to you and thereafter consult with the supervisor about disciplinary actions
   D. deduct three days of annual leave from each employee involved if he pleads guilty in lieu of facing more serious charges

7._____

8. Assume that as a manager you must discipline a subordinate, but all of the pertinent facts necessary for a full determination of the appropriate action to take are not yet available. However, you fear that a delay in disciplinary action may damage the morale of other employees.
   The one of the following which is MOST appropriate for you to do in this matter is to
   A. take immediate disciplinary action as if all the pertinent facts were available
   B. wait until all pertinent facts are available before reaching a decision
   C. inform the subordinate that you know he is guilty, issue a stern warning, and then let him wait for your further action
   D. reduce the severity of the discipline appropriate for the violation

8._____

9. There are two standard dismissal procedures utilized by most public agencies. The first is the "open back door" policy, in which the decision of a supervisor in discharging an employee for reasons of inefficiency cannot be cancelled by the central personnel agency. The second is the "closed back door" policy, in which the central personnel agency can order the supervisor to restore the discharged employee to his position.
   Of the following, the major DISADVANTAGE of the "closed back door" policy as opposed to the "open back door" policy is that central personnel agencies are
   A. likely to approve the dismissal of employees when there is inadequate justification

9._____

B. likely to revoke dismissal actions out of sympathy for employees
  C. less qualified than employing agencies to evaluate the efficiency of employees
  D. easily influenced by political, religious, and racial factors

10. The one of the following for which a formal grievance-handling system is LEAST useful is in
    A. reducing the frequency of employee complaints
    B. diminishing the likelihood of arbitrary action by supervisors
    C. providing an outlet for employee frustrations
    D. bringing employee problems to the attention of higher management

11. The one of the following managers whose leadership style involves the GREATEST delegation of authority to subordinates is the one who presents to subordinates
    A. his ideas and invites questions
    B. his decision and persuades them to accept it
    C. the problem, gets their suggestions, and makes his decision
    D. a tentative decision which is subject to change

12. Which of the following is MOST likely to cause employee productivity standards to be set too high?
    A. Standards of productivity are set by first-line supervisors rather than by higher level managers.
    B. Employees' opinions about productivity standards are sought through written questionnaires.
    C. Initial studies concerning productivity are conducted by staff specialists.
    D. Ideal work conditions assumed in the productivity standards are lacking in actual operations.

13. The one of the following which states the MAIN value of an organization chart for a manager is that such charts show the
    A. lines of formal authority
    B. manner in which duties are performed by each employee
    C. flow of work among employees on the same level
    D. specific responsibilities of each position

14. Which of the following BEST names the usual role of a line unit with regard to the organization's programs?
    A. Seeking publicity   B. Developing
    C. Carrying out   D. Evaluating

15. Critics of promotion *from within* a public agency argue for hiring *from outside* the agency because they believe that promotion from within leads to
    A. resentment and consequent weakened morale on the part of those not promoted
    B. the perpetuation of outdated practices and policies
    C. a more complex hiring procedure than hiring from outside the agency
    D. problems of objectively appraising someone already in the organization

16. The one of the following management functions which usually can be handled MOST effectively by a committee is the
    A. settlement of interdepartmental disputes
    B. planning of routine work schedules
    C. dissemination of information
    D. assignment of personnel

16.____

17. Assume that you are serving on a committee which is considering proposals in order to recommend a new maintenance policy. After eliminating a number of proposals by unanimous consent, the committee is deadlocked on three proposals.
    The one of the following which is the BEST way for the committee to reach agreement on a proposal they could recommend is to
    A. consider and vote on each proposal separately by secret ballot
    B. examine and discuss the three proposals until the proponents of two of them are persuaded they are wrong
    C. reach a synthesis which incorporates the significant features of each proposals
    D. discuss the three proposals until the proponents of each one concede those aspects of the proposals about which there is disagreement

17.____

18. A commonly used training and development method for professional staff is the case method, which utilizes the description of a situation, real or simulated, to provide a common base for analysis, discussion, and problem-solving.
    Of the following, the MOST appropriate time to use the case method is when professional staff needs
    A. insight into their personality problems
    B. practice in applying management concepts to their own problems
    C. practical experience in the assignment of delegated responsibilities
    D. to know how to function in many different capacities

18.____

19. The incident process is a training and development method in which trainees are given a very brief statement of an event or o a situation presenting a job incident or an employee problem of special significance.
    Of the following, it is MOST appropriate to use the incident process when
    A. trainees need to learn to review and analyze facts before solving a problem
    B. there are a large number of trainees who require the same information
    C. there are too many trainees to carry on effective discussion
    D. trainees are not aware of the effect of their behavior on others

19.____

20. The one of the following types of information about which a clerical employee is usually LEAST concerned during the orientation process is
    A. his specific job duties   B. where he will work
    C. his organization's history   D. who his associates will be

20.____

21. The one of the following which is the MOST important limitation on the degree to which work should be broken down into specialized tasks is the point at which
    A. there ceases to be sufficient work of a specialized nature to occupy employees
    B. training costs equal the half-yearly savings derived from further specialization
    C. supervision of employees performing specialized tasks becomes more technical than supervision of general employees
    D. it becomes more difficult to replace the specialist than to replace the generalist who performs a complex set of functions

22. When a supervisor is asked for his opinion of the suitability for promotion of a subordinate, the supervisor is actually being asked to predict the subordinate's future behavior in a new role.
    Such a prediction is MOST likely to be accurate if the
    A. higher position is similar to the subordinate's current one
    B. higher position requires intangible personal qualities
    C. new position has had little personal association with the subordinate away from the job

23. In one form of the non-directive evaluation interview, the supervisor communicates his evaluation to the employee and then listens to the employee's response without making further suggestions.
    The one of the following which is the PRINCIPAL danger of this method of evaluation is that the employee is MOST likely to
    A. develop an indifferent attitude towards the supervisor
    B. fail to discover ways of improving his performance
    C. become resistant to change in the organization's structure
    D. place the blame for his shortcomings on his co-workers

24. In establishing rules for his subordinates, a superior should be PRIMARILY concerned with
    A. creating sufficient flexibility to allow for exceptions
    B. making employees aware of the reasons for the rules and the penalties for infractions
    C. establishing the strength of his own position in relation to his subordinates
    D. having his subordinates know that such rules will be imposed in a personal manner

25. The practice of conducting staff training sessions on a periodic basis is generally considered
    A. *poor*; it takes employees away from their work assignments
    B. *poor*; all staff training should be done on an individual basis
    C. *good*; it permits the regular introduction of new methods and techniques
    D. *good*; it ensures a high employee productivity rate

KEY (CORRECT ANSWERS)

1.	A	11.	C
2.	A	12.	D
3.	A	13.	A
4.	D	14.	C
5.	C	15.	B
6.	B	16.	A
7.	C	17.	C
8.	B	18.	B
9.	C	19.	A
10.	A	20.	C

21. A
22. A
23. B
24. B
25. C

EXAMINATION SECTION

TEST 1

DIRECTIONS: Each question or incomplete statement is followed by several suggested answers or completions. Select the one that BEST answers the question or completes the statement. *PRINT THE LETTER OF THE CORRECT ANSWER IN THE SPACE AT THE RIGHT.*

1. Which one of the following generalizations is MOST likely to be INACCURATE and lead to judgmental errors in communication?   1.____
    A. A supervisor must be able to read with understanding.
    B. Misunderstanding may lead to dislike.
    C. Anyone can listen to another person and understand what he means.
    D. It is usually desirable to let a speaker talk until he is finished.

2. Assume that, as a supervisor, you have been directed to inform your subordinates about the implementation of a new procedure which will affect their work.   2.____
   While communicating this information, you should do all of the following EXCEPT
    A. obtain the approval of your subordinates regarding the new procedure
    B. explain the reason for implementing the new procedure
    C. hold a staff meeting at a time convenient to most of your subordinates
    D. encourage a productive discussion of the new procedure

3. Assume that you are in charge of a section that handles requests for information on matters received from the public. One day, you observe that a clerk under your supervision is using a method to log-in requests for information that is different from the one specified by you in the past. Upon questioning the clerk, you discover that instructions changing the old procedure were delivered orally by your supervisor on a day on which you were absent from the office.   3.____
   Of the following, the MOST appropriate action for you to take is to
    A. tell the clerk to revert to the old procedure at once
    B. ask your supervisor for information about the change
    C. call your staff together and tell them that no existing procedure is to be changed unless you direct that it be done
    D. write a memo to your supervisor suggesting that all future changes in procedure are to be in writing and that they be directed to you

4. At the first meeting with your staff after appointment as a supervisor, you find considerable indifference and some hostility among the participants.   4.____
   Of the following, the MOST appropriate way to handle this situation is to
    A. disregard the attitudes displayed and continue to make your presentation until you have completed it
    B. discontinue your presentation but continue the meeting and attempt to find out the reasons for their attitudes

C. warm up your audience with some good-natured statements and anecdotes and then proceed with your presentation
D. discontinue the meeting and set up personal interviews with the staff members to try to find out the reason for their attitude

5. In order to start the training of a new employee, it has been a standard practice to have him read a manual of instructions or procedures.
   This method is currently being replaced by the _____ method.
   A. audio-visual
   B. conference
   C. lecture
   D. programmed instruction

6. Of the following subjects, the one that can usually be successfully taught by a first-line supervisor who is training his subordinates is:
   A. theory and philosophy of management
   B. human relations
   C. responsibilities of a supervisor
   D. job skills

7. Assume that as supervisor you are training a clerk who is experiencing difficulty learning a new task.
   Which of the following would be the LEAST effective approach to take when trying to solve this problem? To
   A. ask questions which will reveal the clerk's understanding of the task
   B. take a different approach in explaining the task
   C. give the clerk an opportunity to ask questions about the task
   D. make sure the clerk knows you are watching his work closely

8. One school of management and supervision involves participation by employees in the setting of group goals and in the sharing of responsibility for the operation of the unit.
   If this philosophy were applied to a unit consisting of professional and clerical personnel, one should expect
   A. the professional and clerical personnel to participate with equal effectiveness in operating areas and policy areas
   B. the professional personnel to participate with greater effectiveness than the clerical personnel in policy areas
   C. the clerical personnel to participate with greater effectiveness than the professional personnel in operating areas
   D. greater participation by clerical personnel but with less responsibility for their actions

9. With regard to productivity, high morale among employees generally indicates a
   A. history of high productivity
   B. nearly absolute positive correlation with high productivity
   C. predisposition to be productive under facilitating leadership and circumstances
   D. complacency which has little effect on productivity

10. Assume that you are going to organize the professionals and clerks under your supervision into work groups or team of two or three employees.
Of the following, the step which is LEAST likely to foster the successful development of each group is to
    A. allow friends to work together in the group
    B. provide special help and attention to employees with no friends in their group
    C. frequently switch employees from group to group
    D. rotate jobs within the group in order to strengthen group identification

11. Following are four statements which might be made by an employee to his supervisor during a performance evaluation interview.
Which of the statements BEST provides a basis for developing a plan to improve the employee's performance?
    A. *I understand that you are dissatisfied with my work and I will try harder in the future.*
    B. *I feel that I've been making too many careless clerical errors recently.*
    C. *I am aware that I will be subject to disciplinary action if my work does not improve within one month.*
    D. *I understand that this interview is simply a requirement of your job and not a personal attack on me.*

12. Three months ago, Mr. Smith and his supervisor, Mrs. Jones, developed a plan which was intended to correct Mr. Smith's inadequate job performance. Now, during a follow-up interview, Mr. Smith, who thought his performance had satisfactorily improved, has been informed that Mrs. Jones is still dissatisfied with his work.
Of the following, it is MOST likely that the disagreement occurred because, when formulating the plan, they did NOT
    A. set realistic goals for Mr. Smith's performance
    B. set a reasonable time limit for Mr. Smith to effect his improvement in performance
    C. provide for adequate training to improve Mr. Smith's skills
    D. establish performance standards for measuring Mr. Smith's progress

13. When a supervisor delegates authority to subordinates, there are usually many problems to overcome, such as inadequately trained subordinates and poor planning.
All of the following are means of increasing the effectiveness of delegation EXCEPT:
    A. Defining assignments in the light of results expected
    B. Maintaining open lines of communication
    C. Establishing tight controls so that subordinates will stay within the bounds of the area of delegation
    D. Providing rewards for successful assumption of authority by a subordinate

14. Assume that one of your subordinates has arrived late for work several times during the current month. The last time he was late you had warned him that another unexcused lateness would result informal disciplinary action.
If the employee arrives late for work again during this month, the FIRST action you should take is to
    A. give the employee a chance to explain this lateness
    B. give the employee a written copy of your warning
    C. tell the employee that you are recommending formal disciplinary action
    D. tell the employee that you will give him only one more chance before recommending formal disciplinary action

15. In trying to decide how many subordinates a manager can control directly, one of the determinants is how much the manager can reduce the frequency and time consumed in contacts with his subordinates.
Of the following, the factor which LEAST influences the number and direction of these contacts is:
    A. How well the manager delegates authority
    B. The rate at which the organization is changing
    C. The control techniques used by the manager
    D. Whether the activity is line or staff

16. Systematic rotation of employees through lateral transfer within a government organization to provide for managerial development is
    A. *good*, because systematic rotation develops specialists who learn to do many jobs well
    B. *bad*, because the outsider upsets the status quo of the existing organization
    C. *good*, because rotation provides challenge and organizational flexibility
    D. *bad*, because it is upsetting to employees to be transferred within a service

17. Assume that you are required to provide an evaluation of the performance of your subordinates.
Of the following factors, it is MOST important that the performance evaluation include a rating of each employee's
    A. initiative   B. productivity   C. intelligence   D. personality

18. When preparing performance evaluations of your subordinates, one way to help assure that you are rating each employee fairly is to
    A. prepare a list of all employees and all the rating factors and rate all employees on one rating factor before going on to the next factor
    B. prepare a list of all your employees and all the rating factors and rate each employee on all factors before going on to the next employee
    C. discuss all the ratings you anticipate giving with another supervisor in order to obtain an unbiased opinion
    D. discuss each employee with his co-workers in order to obtain peer judgment of worth before doing any rating

19. A managerial plan which would include the GREATEST control is a plan which is
    A. spontaneous and geared to each new job that is received
    B. detailed and covering an extended time period
    C. long-range and generalized, allowing for various interpretations
    D. specific and prepared daily

20. Assume that you are preparing a report which includes statistical data covering increases in budget allocations of four agencies for the past ten years.
    For you to represent the statistical data pictorially or graphically within the report is a
    A. *poor* idea, because you should be able to make statistical data understandable through the use of words
    B. *good* idea, because it is easier for the reader to understand pictorial representation rather than quantities of words conveying statistical data
    C. *poor* idea, because using pictorial representation in a report may make the report too expensive to print
    D. *good* idea, because a pictorial representation makes the report appear more attractive than the use of many words to convey the statistical data

KEY (CORRECT ANSWERS)

1.	C	11.	A
2.	A	12.	B
3.	B	13.	C
4.	D	14.	A
5.	D	15.	D
6.	D	16.	C
7.	D	17.	B
8.	B	18.	A
9.	C	19.	B
10.	C	20.	B

TEST 2

DIRECTIONS: Each question or incomplete statement is followed by several suggested answers or completions. Select the one that BEST answers the question or completes the statement. *PRINT THE LETTER OF THE CORRECT ANSWER IN THE SPACE AT THE RIGHT.*

1. Research studies have shown that supervisors of groups with high production records USUALLY
    A. give detailed instructions, constantly check on progress, and insist on approval of all decisions before implementation
    B. do considerable paperwork and other work similar to that performed by subordinates
    C. think of themselves as team members on the same level as others in the work group
    D. perform tasks traditionally associated with managerial functions

2. Mr. Smith, a bureau chief, is summoned by his agency's head in a conference to discuss Mr. Jones, an accountant who works in one of the divisions of his bureau. Mr. Jones has committed an error of such magnitude as to arouse the agency head's concern.
   After agreeing with the other conferees that a severe reprimand would be the appropriate punishment, Mr. Smith SHOULD
    A. arrange for Mr. Jones to explain the reasons for his error to the agency head
    B. send a memorandum to Mr. Jones, being careful that the language emphasizes the nature of the error rather than Mr. Jones' personal faults
    C. inform Mr. Jones' immediate supervisor of the conclusion reached at the conference, and let the supervisor take the necessary action
    D. suggest to the agency head that no additional action be taken against Mr. Jones because no further damage will be caused by the error

3. Assume that Ms. Thomson, a unit chief, has determined that the findings of an internal audit have been seriously distorted as a result of careless errors. The audit had been performed by a group of auditors in her unit and the errors were overlooked by the associate accountant in charge of the audit. Ms. Thomson has decided to delay discussing the matter with the associate accountant and the staff who performed the audit until she verifies certain details, which may require prolonged investigation.
   Mrs. Thomson's method of handling this situation is
    A. *appropriate*; employees should not be accused of wrongdoing until all the facts have been determined
    B. *inappropriate*; the employees involved may assume that the errors were considered unimportant
    C. *appropriate*; employees are more likely to change their behavior as a result of disciplinary action taken after a *cooling off* period
    D. *inappropriate*; the employees involved may have forgotten the details and become emotionally upset when confronted with the facts

4. After studying the financial situation in his agency, an administrative accountant decides to recommend centralization of certain accounting functions which are being performed in three different bureaus of the organization
   The one of the following which is MOST likely to be a DISADVANTAE if this recommendation is implemented is that
   A. there may be less coordination of the accounting procedure because central direction is not so close to the day-to-day problems as the personnel handling them in each specialized accounting unit
   B. the higher management levels would not be able to make emergency decisions in as timely a manner as the more involved, lower-level administrators who are closer to the problem
   C. it is more difficult to focus the attention of the top management in order to resolve accounting problems because of the many other activities top management is involved in at the same time
   D. the accuracy of upward and inter-unit communication may be reduced because centralization may require insertion of more levels of administration in the chain of command

5. Of the following assumptions about the role of conflict in an organization, the one which is the MOST accurate statement of the approach of modern management theorists is that conflict
   A. can usually be avoided or controlled
   B. serves as a vital element in organizational change
   C. works against attainment of organizational goals
   D. provides a constructive outlet for problem employees

6. Which of the following is generally regarded as the BEST approach for a supervisor to follow in handling grievances brought by subordinates?
   A. Avoid becoming involved personally
   B. Involve the union representative in the first stage of discussion
   C. Settle the grievance as soon as possible
   D. Arrange for arbitration by a third party

7. Assume that supervisors of similar-sized accounting units in city, state, and federal offices were interviewed and observed at their work. It was found that the ways they acted in and viewed their roles tended to be very similar, regardless of who employed them.
   Which of the following is the BEST explanation of this similarity
   A. A supervisor will ordinarily behave in conformance to his own self-image.
   B. Each role in an organization, including the supervisory role, calls for a distinct type of personality.
   C. The supervisor role reflects an exceptionally complex pattern of human response.
   D. The general nature of the duties and responsibilities of the supervisory position determines the role.

8. Which of the following is NOT consistent with the findings of recent research about the characteristics of successful top managers?
    A. They are *inner-directed* and not overly concerned with pleasing others.
    B. They are challenged by situations filled with high risk and ambiguity.
    C. They tend to stay on the same job for long periods of time.
    D. They consider it more important to handle critical assignments successfully than to do routine work well.

9. As a supervisor, you have to give subordinates operational guidelines. Of the following, the BEST reason for providing them with information about the overall objectives within which their operations fit is that the subordinates will
    A. be more likely to carry out the operation according to your expectations
    B. know that there is a legitimate reason for carrying out the operation in the way you have prescribed
    C. be more likely to handle unanticipated problems that may arise without having to take up your time
    D. more likely to transmit the operating instructions correctly to their subordinates

10. A supervisor holds frequent meetings with his staff. Of the following, the BEST approach he can take in order to elicit productive discussions at these meetings is for him to
    A. ask questions of those who attend
    B. include several levels of supervisors at the meetings
    C. hold the meetings at a specified time each week
    D. begin each meeting with a statement that discussion is welcomed

11. Of the following, the MOST important action that a supervisor can take to increase the productivity of a subordinate is to
    A. increase his uninterrupted work time
    B. increase the number of reproducing machines available in the office
    C. provide clerical assistance whenever he requests it
    D. reduce the number of his assigned tasks

12. Assume that, as a supervisor, you find out that you often must countermand or modify your original staff memos.
    If this practice continues, which one of the following situations is MOST likely to occur? The
    A. staff will not bother to read your memos
    B. office files will become cluttered
    C. staff will delay acting on your memos
    D. memos will be treated routinely

13. In making management decisions, the committee approach is often used by managers.
    Of the following, the BEST reason for using this approach is to
    A. prevent any one individual from assuming too much authority
    B. allow the manager to bring a wider range of experience and judgment to bear on the problem

C. allow the participation of all staff members, which will make them feel more committed to the decisions reached
D. permit the rapid transmission of information about decisions reached to the staff members concerned

14. In establishing standards for the measurement of the performance of a management project team, it is MOST important for the project manager to
    A. identify and define the objectives of the project
    B. determine the number of people who will be assigned to the project team
    C. evaluate the skills of the staff who will be assigned to the project team
    D. estimate fairly accurately the length of time required to complete each phase of the project

15. It is virtually impossible to tell an employee either that he is not good as another employee or that he does not measure up to a desirable level of performance, without having him feel threatened, rejected, and discouraged.
    In accordance with the foregoing observation, a supervisor who is concerned about the performance of the less efficient members of his staff should realize that
    A. he might obtain better results by not discussing the quality and quantity of their work with them, but by relying instead on the written evaluation of their performance to motivate their improvement
    B. since he is required to discuss their performance with them, he should do so in words of encouragement and in so friendly a manner as to not destroy their morale
    C. he might discuss their work in a general way, without mentioning any of the specifics about the quality of their performance, with the expectation that they would understand the full implications of his talk
    D. he should make it a point, while telling them of their poor performance, to mention that their work is as good as that of some of the other employees in the unit

16. Some advocates of management-by-objectives procedures in public agencies have been urging that this method of operations be expanded to encompass all agencies of the government, for one or more of the following reasons, not all of which may be correct:
    I. The MBO method is likely to succeed because it embraces the practice of setting near-term goals for the subordinate manager, reviewing accomplishments at an appropriate time, and repeating this process indefinitely
    II. Provision for authority to perform the tasks assigned as goals in the MBO method is normally not needed because targets are set in quantitative or qualitative terms and specific times for accomplishment are arranged in short-term, repetitive intervals
    III. Many other appraisal-of-performance programs failed because both supervisors and subordinates resisted them, while the MBO approach is not instituted until there is an organizational commitment to it
    IV. Personal accountability is clearly established through the MBO approach because verifiable results are set up in the process of formulating the targets

Which of the choices below includes ALL of the foregoing statements that are CORRECT?
A. I, III B. II, IV C. I, II, III, IV D. I, III, IV

17. In preparing an organizational structure, the PRINCIPAL guideline for locating staff units is to place them
    A. all under a common supervisor
    B. as close as possible to the activities they serve
    C. as close to the chief executive as possible without over-extending his span of control
    D. at the lowest operational level

18. The relative importance of any unit in a department can be LEAST reliably judged by the
    A. amount of office space allocated to the unit
    B. number of employees in the unit
    C. rank of the individual who heads the unit
    D. rank of the individual to whom the unit head reports directly

19. Those who favor Planning-Programming-Budgeting Systems (PPBS) as a new method of governmental financial administration emphasize that PPBS
    A. applies statistical measurements which correlate highly with criteria
    B. makes possible economic systems analysis, including an explicit examination of alternatives
    C. makes available scarce government resources which can be coordinated on a government-wide basis and shared between local units of government
    D. shifts the emphasis in budgeting methods to an automated system of data processing

20. The term applied to computer processing which processes data concurrently with a given activity and provides results soon enough to influence the selection of a course of action is _____ processing.
    A. realtime   B. batch
    C. random access   D. integrated data

6 (#2)

KEY (CORRECT ANSWERS)

1.	D	11.	A
2.	C	12.	C
3.	B	13.	B
4.	D	14.	A
5.	B	15.	B
6.	C	16.	D
7.	D	17.	B
8.	C	18.	B
9.	C	19.	B
10.	A	20.	A

PREPARING WRITTEN MATERIAL

PARAGRAPH REARRANGEMENT
COMMENTARY

The sentences that follow are in scrambled order. You are to rearrange them in proper order and indicate the letter choice containing the correct answer at the space at the right.

Each group of sentences in this section is actually a paragraph presented in scrambled order. Each sentence in the group has a place in that paragraph; no sentence is to be left out. You are to read each group of sentences and decide upon the best order in which to put the sentences so as to form a well-organized paragraph.

The questions in this section measure the ability to solve a problem when all the facts relevant to its solution are not given.

More specifically, certain positions of responsibility and authority require the employee to discover connection between events sometimes, apparently, unrelated. In order to do this, the employee will find it necessary to correctly infer that unspecified events have probably occurred or are likely to occur. This ability becomes especially important when action must be taken on incomplete information.

Accordingly, these questions require competitors to choose among several suggested alternatives, each of which presents a different sequential arrangement of the events. Competitors must choose the MOST logical of the suggested sequences.

In order to do so, they may be required to draw on general knowledge to infer missing concepts or events that are essential to sequencing the given events. Competitors should be careful to infer only what is essential to the sequence. The plausibility of the wrong alternatives will always require the inclusion of unlikely events or of additional chains of events which are NOT essential to sequencing the given events.

It's very important to remember that you are looking for the best of the four possible choices, and that the best choice of all may not even be one of the answers you're given to choose from.

There is no one right way to solve these problems. Many people have found it helpful to first write out the order of the sentences, as they would have arranged them, on their scrap paper before looking at the possible answers. If their optimum answer is there, this can save them some time. If it isn't, this method can still give insight into solving the problem. Others find it most helpful to just go through each of the possible choices, contrasting each as they go along. You should use whatever method feels comfortable and works for you.

While most of these types of questions are not that difficult, we've added a higher percentage of the difficult type, just to give you more practice. Usually there are only one or two questions on this section that contain such subtle distinctions that you're unable to answer confidently. And you then may find yourself stuck deciding between two possible choices, neither of which you're sure about.

PREPARING WRITTEN MATERIAL
PARAGRAPH REARRANGEMENT
EXAMINATION SECTION
TEST 1

DIRECTIONS: The following groups of sentences need to be arranged in an order that makes sense. Select the letter preceding the sequence that represents the best sentence order. *PRINT THE LETTER OF THE CORRECT ANSWER IN THE SPACE AT THE RIGHT.*

1.
   I. The ostrich egg shell's legendary toughness makes it an excellent substitute for certain types of dishes or dinnerware, and in parts of Africa ostrich shells are cut and decorated for use as containers for water.
   II. Since prehistoric times, people have used the enormous egg of the ostrich as a part of their diet, a practice which has required much patience and hard work—to hard boil an ostrich egg takes about four hours.
   III. Opening the egg's shell, which is rock hard and nearly an inch thick, requires heavy tools, such as a saw or chisel; from inside, a baby ostrich must use a hornlike projection on its beak as a miniature pick-axe to escape from the egg.
   IV. The offspring of all higher-order animals originate from single egg cells that are carried by mothers, and most of these eggs are relatively small, often microscopic.
   V. The egg of the African ostrich, however, weighs a massive thirty pounds, making it the largest single cell on earth, and a common object of human curiosity and wonder.

   The BEST order is:
   A. V, IV, I, II, III   B. I, IV, V, III, II   C. IV, II, III, V, I   D. IV, V, II, III, I

   1.____

2.
   I. Typically only a few feet high on the open sea, individual tsunami have been known to circle the entire globe two or three times if their progress is not interrupted, but are not usually dangerous until they approach the shallow water that surrounds land masses.
   II. Some of the most terrifying and damaging hazards caused by earthquakes are tsunami, which were once called "tidal waves"—a poorly chosen name, since these waves have nothing to do with tides.
   III. Then a wave, slowed by the sudden drag on the lower part of its moving water column, will pile upon itself, sometimes reaching a height of over 100 feet.
   IV. Tsunami (Japanese for "great harbor wave") are seismic waves that are caused by earthquakes near oceanic trenches, and once triggered, can travel up to 600 miles an hour on the open ocean.
   V. A land-shoaling tsunami is capable of extraordinary destruction; some tsunami have deposited large boats miles inland, washed out two-foot-thick seawalls, and scattered locomotive trains over long distances.

   The BEST order is:
   A. IV, I, III, II, V   B. I, III, IV, II, V   C. V, I, III, II, IV   D. II, IV, I, III, V

   2.____

3. I. Soon, by the 1940s, jazz was the most popular type of music among American intellectuals and college students.
    II. In the early days of jazz, it was considered "lowdown" music, or music that was played only in rough, disreputable bars and taverns.
    III. However, jazz didn't take too long to develop from early ragtime melodies into more complex, sophisticated forms, such as Charlie Parker's "bebop" style of jazz.
    IV. After charismatic band leaders such as Duke Ellington and Count Basie brought jazz to a larger audience, and jazz continued to evolve into more complicated forms, white audiences began to accept and even to enjoy the new American art form.
    V. Many white Americans, who then dictated the tastes of society, were wary of music that was played almost exclusively in black clubs in the poorer sections of cities and towns.
    The BEST order is:
    A. V, IV, III, II, I   B. II, V, III, IV, I   C. IV, V, III, I, II   D. I, II, IV, III, V

4. I. Then, hanging in a windless place, the magnetized end of the needle would always point to the south.
    II. The needle could then be balanced on the rim of a cup, or the edge of a fingernail, but this balancing act was hard to maintain, and the needle often fell off.
    III. Other needles would point to the north, and it was important for any traveler finding his way with a compass to remember which kind of magnetized needle he was carrying.
    IV. To make some of the earliest compasses in recorded history, ancient Chinese "magicians" would rub a needle with a piece of magnetized iron called a lodestone.
    V. A more effective method of keeping the needle free to swing with its magnetic pull was to attach a strand of silk to the center of the needle with a tiny piece of wax.
    The BEST order is:
    A. IV, II, V, I, III   B. IV, III, V, II, I   C. IV, V, II, I, III   D. IV, I, III, V, II

5. I The now-famous first mate of the *H.M.S. Bounty*, Fletcher Christian, founded one of the world's most peculiar civilizations in 1790.
    II. The men knew they had just committed a crime for which they could be hanged, so they set sail for Pitcairn, a remote, abandoned island in the far eastern region of the Polynesian archipelago, accompanied by twelve Polynesian women and six men.
    III. In a mutiny that has become legendary, Christian and the others forced Captain Bligh into a lifeboat and set him adrift off the coast of Tonga in April of 1789.
    IV. In early 1790, the *Bounty* landed at Pitcairn Island, where the men lived out the rest of their lives and founded an isolated community which to this day includes direct descendants of Christian and the other Crewmen.

V. The *Bounty*, commanded by Captain William Bligh, was in the middle of a global voyage, and Christian and his shipmates had come to the conclusion that Bligh was a reckless madman who would lead them to their deaths unless they took the ship from him.

The BEST order is:
   A. IV, V, III, II, I   B. I, III, V, II, IV   C. I, V, III, II, IV   D. III, I, V, IV, II

6.   I. But once the vines had been led to make orchids, the flowers had to be carefully hand-pollinated, because unpollinated orchids usually lasted less than a day, wilting and dropping off the vine before it had even become dark.
   II. The Totonac farmers discovered that looping a vine back around once it reached a five-foot height on its host tree would cause the vine to flower.
   III. Though they knew how to process the fruit pods and extract vanilla's flavoring agent, the Totonacs also knew that a wild vanilla vine did not produce abundant flowers or fruit.
   IV. Wild vines climbed along the trunks and canopies of trees, and this constant upward growth diverted most of the vine's energy to making leaves instead of the orchid flowers that once pollinated, would produce the flavorful pods.
   V. Hundreds of years before vanilla became a prized food flavoring in Europe and the Western World, the Totonac Indians of the Mexican Gulf Coast were skilled cultivators of the vanilla vine, whose fruit they literally worshipped as a goddess.

The BEST order is:
   A. II, III, IV, I, V   B. II, IV, III, I, V   C. V, III, IV, II, I   D. III, IV, I, II, V

7.   I. Once airborne, the spider is at the mercy of the air currents—usually the spider takes a brief journey, traveling close to the ground, but some have been found in air samples collected as high as 10,000 feet, or been reported landing on ships far out at sea.
   II. Once a young spider has hatched, it must leave the environment into which it was born as quickly as possible, in order to avoid competing with its hundreds of brothers and sisters for food.
   III. The silk rises into warm air currents, and as soon as the pull feels adequate the spider lets go and drifts up into the air, suspended from the silk strand in the same way that a person might parasail.
   IV. To help young spiders do this, many species have adapted a practice known as "aerial dispersal," or, in common speech, "ballooning."
   V. A spider that wants to leave its surroundings quickly will climb to the top of a grass system or twig, face into the wind, and aim its back end into the air, releasing a long stream of silk from the glands near the tip of its abdomen.

The BEST order is:
   A. V, IV, II, III, I   B. V, II, IV, I, III   C. II, V, IV, III, I   D. II, IV, V, III, I

8. I. For about a year, Tycho worked at a castle in Prague with a scientist named Johannes Kepler, but their association was cut short by another argument that drove Kepler out of the castle, to later develop, on his own, the theory of planetary orbits.
    II. Tycho found life without a nose embarrassing, so he made a new nose for himself out of silver, which reportedly remained glued to his face for the rest of his life.
    III. Tycho Brahe, the 17th-century Danish astronomer, is today more famous for his odd and arrogant personality than for any contribution he has made to our knowledge of the stars and planets.
    IV. Early in his career, as a student at Rostock University, Tycho got into an argument with another student about who was the better mathematician, and the two became so angry that the argument turned into a sword fight, during which Tycho's nose was sliced off.
    V. Later in his life, Tycho's arrogance may have kept him from playing a part in one of the greatest astronomical discoveries in history: the elliptical orbits of the solar system's planets.

    The BEST order is:
    A. I, IV, II, III, V   B. IV, II, III, V, I   C. IV, II, I, III, V   D. III, IV, II, V, I

9. I. The processionaries are so used to this routine that if a person picks up the end of a silk line and brings it back to the origin—creating a closed circle—the caterpillars may travel around and around for days, sometimes starving or freezing, without changing course.
    II. Rather than relying on sight or sound, the other caterpillars, who are lined up end-to-end behind the leader, travel to and from their nests by walking on this silk line, and each will reinforce it by laying down its own marking line as it passes over.
    III. In order to insure the safety of individuals, the processionary caterpillar nests in a tree with dozens of other caterpillars, and at night, when it is safest, they all leave together in search of food.
    IV. The processionary caterpillar of the European continent is a perfect illustration of how much some inspect species rely on instinct in their daily routines.
    V. As they leave their nests, the processionaries form a single-file line behind a leader who spins and lays out a silk line to mark the chosen path.

    The BEST order is:
    A. IV, III, V, II, I   B. III, V, IV, II, I   C. III, V, II, I, IV   D. IV, V, III, I, II

10. I. Often, the child is also given a handcrafted walker or push cart, to provide support for its first upright explorations.
    II. In traditional Indian families, a child's first steps are celebrated as a ceremonial event, rooted in ancient myth.
    III. These carts are often intricately designed to resemble the chariot of Krishna, an important figure in Indian mythology.
    IV. The sound of these anklet bells is intended to mimic the footsteps of the legendary child Rama, who is celebrated in devotional songs throughout India.

V. When the child's parents see that the child is ready to begin walking, they will fit it with specially designed ankle bracelets, adorned with gently ringing bells.

The BEST order is:
A. II, III, IV, I, V   B. II, V, III, I, IV   C. V, IV, I, III, II   D. V, III, II, I, IV

11.
I. The settlers planted Osage oranges all across Middle America, and today long lines and rectangles of Osage orange trees can still be seen on the prairies, running along the former boundaries of farms that no longer exist.
II. After trying sod walls and water-filled ditches with no success, American farmers began to look for a plant that was adaptable to prairie weather, and that could be trimmed into a hedge that was "pig-tight, horse-high, and bull-strong."
III. The tree, so named because it bore a large (but inedible) fruit the size of an orange, was among the sturdiest and hardiest of American trees, and was prized among Native Americans for the strength and flexibility of bows which were made from its wood.
IV. The first people to practice agriculture on the American flatlands were faced with an important problem: what would they use to fence their land in a place that was almost entirely without trees or rocks?
V. Finally, an Illinois farmer brought the settlers a tree that was native to the land between the Red and Arkansas rivers, a tree called the Osage orange.

The BEST order is:
A. II, I, V, III, IV   B. I, II, III, IV, V   C. IV, II, V, III, I   D. IV, II, I, III, V

12.
I. After about ten minutes of such spirited and complicated activity, the head dancer is free to make up his or her own movements while maintaining the interest of the New Year's crowd.
II. The dancer will then perform a series of leg kicks, while at the same time operating the lion's mouth with his own hand and moving the ears and eyes by means of a string which is attached to the dancer's own mouth.
III. The most difficult role of this dance belongs to the one who controls the lion's head; this person must lead all the other "parts" of the lion through the choreographed segments of the dance.
IV. The head dancer begins with a complex series of steps. alternately stepping forward with the head raised, and then retreating a few steps while lowering the head, a movement that is intended to create the impression that the lion is keeping a watchful eye for anything evil.
V. When performing a traditional Chinese New Year's lion dance, several performers must fit themselves inside a large lion costume and work together to enact different parts of the dance.

The BEST order is:
A. V, III, IV, II, I   B. III, IV, II, V, I   C. III, I, V, IV, II   D. IV, II, III, V, I

13. I. For many years the shell of the chambered nautilus was treasured in Europe for its beauty and intricacy, but collectors were unaware that they were in possession of the structure that marked a "missing link" in the evolution of marine mollusks.
II. The nautilus, however, evolved a series of enclosed chambers in its shell, and invented a new use for the structure: the shell began to serve as a buoyancy device.
III. Equipped with this new flotation device, the nautilus did not need the single, muscular foot of its predecessors, but instead developed flaps, tentacles, and a gentle form of jet propulsion that transformed it into the first mollusk able to take command of its own density and explore a three-dimensional world.
IV. By pumping and adjusting air pressure into the chambers, the nautilus could spend the day resting on the bottom, and then rise toward the surface at night in search of food.
V. The nautilus shell looks like a large snail shell, similar to those of its ancestors, who used their shells as protective coverings while they were anchored to the sea floor.
The BEST order is:
  A. V, II, IV, I, III   B. V, I, II, III, IV   C. I, II, V, III, IV   D. I, V, II, IV, III

13.____

14. I. While France and England battled for control of the region, the Acadiens prospered on the fertile farmland, which was finally secured by England in 1713.
II. Early in the 17th century, settlers from Western France founded a colony called Acadie in what is now the Canadian province of Nova Scotia.
III. At this time, English officials feared the presence of spies among the Acadiens who might be loyal to their French homeland, and the Acadiens were deported to spots along the Atlantic and Caribbean shores of America.
IV. The French settlers remained on this land, under English rule, for around forty years, until the beginning of the French and Indian War, another conflict between France and England.
V. As the Acadien refugees drifted toward a final home in Southern Louisiana, neighbors shortened their name to "Cadien," and finally "Cajun," the name which the descendants of early Acadiens still call themselves.
The BEST order is:
  A. I, IV, II, III, V   B. II, I, III, V, IV   C. II, I, IV, III, V   D. V, II, III, IV, I

14.____

15. I. Traditional households in the Eastern and Western regions of Africa serve two meals a day—one at around noon, and the other in the evening.
II. The starch is then used in the way that Americans might use a spoon, to scoop up a portion of the main dish on the person's plate.
III. The reason for the starch's inclusion in every meal has to do with taste as well as nutrition; African food can be very spicy, and the starch is known to cool the burning effect of the main dish.
IV. When serving these meals, the main dish is usually served on individual plates, and the starch is served on a communal plate, from which diners break off a piece of bread or scoop rice or fufu in their fingers.

15.____

V. The typical meals usually consist of a thick stew or soup as the main course, and an accompanying starch—either bread, rice, or *fufu*, a starchy grain paste similar in consistency to mashed potatoes.

The BEST order is:
A. V, II, III, IV, I   B. V, I, IV, III, II   C. I, IV, V, III, II   D. I, V, IV, II, III

16. I. In the early days of the American Midwest, Indiana settlers sometimes came together to hold an event called an apple peeling, where neighboring settlers gathered at the homestead of a host family to help prepare the hosts' apple crop for cooking, canning, and making apple butter.
    II. At the beginning of the event, each peeler sat down in front of a ten- or twenty-gallon stone jar and was given a crock of apples and a paring knife.
    III. Once a peeler had finished with a crock, another was placed next to him; if the peeler was an unmarried man, he kept a strict count of the number of apples he had peeled, because the winner was allowed to kiss the girl of his choice.
    IV. The peeling usually ended by 9:30 in the evening, when the neighbors gathered in the host family's parlor for a dance social.
    V. The apples were peeled, cored, and quartered, and then placed into the jar.

    The BEST order is:
    A. I, V, III, IV, II   B. II, V, III, IV, I   C. I, II, V, III, IV   D. II, I, V, IV, III

17. I. If your pet turtle is a land turtle and is native to temperate climates, it will stop eating some time in October, which should be your cue to prepare the turtle for hibernation.
    II. The box should then be covered with a wire screen, which will protect the turtle from any rodents or predators that might want to take advantage of a motionless and helpless animal.
    III. When your turtle hasn't eaten for a while and appears ready to hibernate, it should be moved to its winter quarters, most likely a cellar or garage, where the temperature should range between 40° and 45°F.
    IV. Instead of feeding the turtle, you should bathe it every day in warm water, to encourage the turtle to empty its intestines in preparation for its long winter sleep.
    V. Here the turtle should be placed in a well-ventilated box whose bottom is covered with a moisture-absorbing layer of clay beads, and then filled three-fourths full with almost dry peat moss or wood chips, into which the turtle will burrow and sleep for several months.

    The BEST order is:
    A. I, IV, III, V, II   B. III, IV, II, V, I   C. III, II, IV, I, V   D. IV, V, II, III, I

18. I. Once he has reached the nest, the hunter uses two sturdy bamboo poles like huge chopsticks to pull the next away from the mountainside, into a large basket that will be lowered to people waiting below.
    II. The world's largest honeybees colonize the Nealese mountainsides, building honeycombs as large as a person on sheer rock faces that are often hundreds of feet high.

III. In the remote mountain country of Nepal, a small band of "honey hunters" carry out a tradition so ancient that 10,000 year-old drawings of the practice have been found in the caves of Nepal.
IV. To harvest the honey and beeswax from these combs, a honey hunter climbs above the nests, lowers a long bamboo-fiber ladder over the cliff, and then climbs down.
V. Throughout this dangerous practice, the hunter is stung repeatedly, and only the veterans, with skin that has been toughened over the years, are able to return from a hunt without the painful swelling caused by stings.

The BEST order is:
A. II, IV, III, V, I   B. II, IV, I, V, III   C. V, III, II, IV, I   D. III, II, IV, I, V

19. I. After the Romans left Britain, there were relentless attacks on the islands from the barbarian tribes of northern Germany—the Angles, Saxons, and Jutes.
    II. As the empire weakened, Roman soldiers withdrew from Britain, leaving behind a country that continued to practice the Christian religion that had been introduced by the Romans.
    III. Early Latin writings tell of a Christian warrior named Arturius (Arthur, in English) who led the British citizens to defeat these barbarian invades, and brought an extended period of peace to the lands of Britain.
    IV. Long ago, the British Isles were part of the far-flung Roman Empire that extended across most of Europe and into Africa and Asia.
    V. The romantic legend of King Arthur and his knights of the Round Table, one of the most popular and widespread stories of all time, appears to have some foundation in history.

    The BEST order is:
    A. V, IV, III, II, I   B. V, IV, II, I, III   C. IV, V, II, III, I   D. IV, III, II, I, V

19.____

20. I. The cylinder was allowed to cool until it could stand on its own, and then it was cut from the tube and split down the side with a single straight cut.
    II. Nineteenth-century glassmakers, who had not yet discovered the glazier's modern techniques for making panes of glass, had to create a method for converting their blown gas into flat sheets.
    III. The bubble was then pierced at the end to make a hole that opened up while the glassmaker gently spun it, creating a cylinder of glass.
    IV. Turned on its side and laid on a conveyor belt, the cylinder was strengthened, or tempered, by being heated again and cooled very slowly, eventually flattening out into a single rectangular of glass.
    V. To do this, the glassmaker dipped the end of a long tube into melted glass and blew into the other end of the tube, creating an expanding bubble of glass.

    The BEST order is:
    A. II, V, III, IV, I   B. II, IV, V, III, I   C. III, V, II, IV, I   D. III, I, IV, V, II

20.____

21. I. The splints are almost always hidden, but horses are occasionally born whose splinted toes project from the leg on either side, just above the hoof.
    II. The second and fourth toes remained, but shrank to thin splints of bone that fused invisibly to the horse's leg bone.
    III. Horses are unique among mammals, having evolved feet that each end in what is essentially a single toe, capped by a large, sturdy hoof.
    IV. Julius Caesar, an emperor of ancient Rome, was said to have owned one of these three-toed horses, and considered it so special that he would not permit anyone else to ride it.
    V. Though the horse's earlier ancestors possessed the traditional mammalian set of five toes on each foot, the horse has retained only its third toe; its first and fifth toes disappeared completely as the horse evolved.
    The BEST order is:
       A. III, V, II, I, IV   B. V, III, II, IV, I   C. III, II, V, I, IV   D. V, II, III, I, IV

22. I. The new building materials—some of which are twenty feet long, and weigh nearly six tons—were transported to Pohnpei on rafts, and were brought into their present position by using hibiscus fiber ropes and leverage to move the stone columns upward along the inclined trunks of coconut palm trees.
    II. The ancestors built great fires to heat the stone, and then poured cool seawater on the columns, which caused the stone to contract and split along natural fracture lines.
    III. The now-abandoned enclave of Nan Madol, a group of 92 man-made islands off the shore of the Micronesian island of Pohnpei, is estimated to have been built around the year 500 A.D.
    IV. The islanders say their ancestors quarried stone columns from a nearby island, where large basalt columns were formed by the cooling of molten lava.
    V. The structures of Nan Madol are remarkable for the sheer size of some of the stone "longs" or columns that were used to create the walls of the offshore community, and today anthropologists can only rely on the information of existing local people for clues about how Nan Madol was built.
    The BEST order is:
       A. V, IV, III, II, I   B. V, III, I, IV, II   C. III, V, IV, II, I   D. III, I, IV, II, V

23. I. One of the most easily manipulated substances on earth, glass can be made into ceramic tiles that are composed of over 90% air.
    II. NASA's space shuttles are the first spacecraft ever designed to leave and re-enter the earth's atmosphere while remaining intact.
    III. These ceramic tiles are such effective insulators that when a tile emerges from the oven in which it was fired, it can be held safely in a person's hand by the edges while its interior still glows at a temperature well over 2000°F.
    IV. Eventually, the engineers were led to a material that is as old as our most ancient civilization.
    V. Because the temperature during atmospheric re-entry is so incredibly hot, it took NASA's engineers some time to find a substance capable of protecting the shuttles.

The BEST order is:
A. V, II, I, II, IV B. II, V, IV, I, III C. II, III, I, IV, V D. V, IV, III, I, II

24. I. The secret to teaching any parakeet to talk is patience, and the understanding that when a bird talks," it is simply imitating what it hears, rather than putting ideas into words.
II. You should stay just out of sight of the bird and repeat the phrase you want it to learn, for at least fifteen minutes every morning and evening.
III. It is important to leave the bird without any words of encouragement or farewell; otherwise it might combine stray remarks or phrases, such as "Good night," with the phrase you are trying to teach it.
IV. For this reason, to train your bird to imitate your words you should keep it free of any distractions, especially other noises, while you are giving it "lesson."
V. After your repetition, you should quietly leave the bird alone for a while, to think over what it has just heard.
The BEST order is:
A. I, IV, II, V, III B. I, II, IV, III, V C. III, II, I, V, IV D. III, I, V, IV, II

24.____

25. I. As a school approaches, fishermen from neighboring communities join their fishing boats together as a fleet, and string their gill nets together to make a huge fence that is held up by cork floats.
II. At a signal from the party leaders, or *nakura*, the family members pound the sides of the boats or beat the water with long poles, creating a sudden and deafening noise.
III. The fishermen work together to drag the trap into a half-circle that may reach 300 yards in diameter, and then the families move their boats to form the other half of the circle around the school of fish.
IV. The school of fish flee from the commotion into the awaiting trap, where a final wall of net is thrown over the open end of the half-circle, securing the day's haul.
V. Indonesian people from the area around the Sulu islands live on the sea, in floating villages made of lashed-together or stilted homes, and make much of their living by fishing their home waters for migrating schools of snapper, scad, and other fish.
The BEST order is:
A. I, V, III, IV, II B. I, II, IV, III, V C. V, I, II, III, IV D. V, I, III, II, IV

25.____

KEY (CORRECT ANSWERS)

1.	D	11.	C
2.	D	12.	A
3.	B	13.	D
4.	A	14.	C
5.	C	15.	D
6.	C	16.	C
7.	D	17.	A
8.	D	18.	D
9.	A	19.	B
10.	B	20.	A

21. A
22. C
23. B
24. A
25. D

PREPARING WRITTEN MATERIAL
EXAMINATION SECTION
TEST 1

DIRECTIONS: Each question consists of a sentence which may or may not be an example of good English usage. Examine each sentence, considering grammar, punctuation, spelling, capitalization, and awkwardness. Then choose the correct statement about it from the four choices below it. If the English usage in the sentence given is better than any of the changes suggested in choices B, C, or D, pick choice A. (Do not pick a choice that will change the meaning of the sentence.) *PRINT THE LETTER OF THE CORRECT ANSWER IN THE SPACE AT THE RIGHT.*

1. We attended a staff conference on Wednesday the new safety and fire rules were discussed. 1.____
   A. This is an example of acceptable writing.
   B. The words "safety," "fire," and "rules" should begin with capital letters.
   C. There should be a comma after the word "Wednesday."
   D. There should be a period after the word "Wednesday" and the word "the" should begin with a capital letter.

2. Neither the dictionary or the telephone directory could be found in the office library. 2.____
   A. This is an example of acceptable writing.
   B. The word "or" should be changed to "nor."
   C. The word "library" should be spelled "libery."
   D. The word "neither" should be changed to "either."

3. The report would have been typed correctly if the typist could read the draft. 3.____
   A. This is an example of acceptable writing.
   B. The word "would" should be removed.
   C. The word "have" should be inserted after the word "could."
   D. The word "correctly" should be changed to "correct."

4. The supervisor brought the reports and forms to an employees desk. 4.____
   A. This is an example of acceptable writing.
   B. The word "brought" should be changed to "took."
   C. There should be a comma after the word "reports" and a comma after the word "forms."
   D. The word "employees" should be spelled "employee's."

5. It's important for all the office personnel to submit their vacation schedules on time. 5.____
   A. This is an example of acceptable writing.
   B. The word "It's" should be spelled "Its."
   C. The word "their" should be spelled "they're."
   D. The word "personnel" should be spelled "personal."

125

6. The report, along with the accompanying documents, were submitted for review. 6._____
   A. This is an example of acceptable writing.
   B. The words "were submitted" should be changed to "was submitted."
   C. The word "accompanying" should be spelled "accompaning."
   D. The comma after the word "report" should be taken out.

7. If others must use your files, be certain that they understand how the system works, but insist that you do all the filing and refiling. 7._____
   A. This is an example of acceptable writing.
   B. There should be a period after the word "works," and the word "but" should start a new sentence.
   C. The words "filing" and "refiling" should be spelled "fileing" and "refileing."
   D. There should be a comma after the word "but."

8. The appeal was not considered because of its late arrival. 8._____
   A. This is an example of acceptable writing.
   B. The word "its" should be changed to "it's."
   C. The word "its" should be changed to "the."
   D. The words "late arrival" should be changed to "arrival late."

9. The letter must be read carefuly to determine under which subject it should be filed. 9._____
   A. This is an example of acceptable writing.
   B. The word "under" should be changed to "at."
   C. The word "determine" should be spelled "determin."
   D. The word "carefuly" should be spelled "carefully."

10. He showed potential as an office manager, but he lacked skill in delegating work. 10._____
    A. This is an example of acceptable writing.
    B. The word "delegating" should be spelled "delagating."
    C. The word "potential" should be spelled "potencial."
    D. The words "he lacked" should be changed to "was lacking."

KEY (CORRECT ANSWERS)

1.	D	6.	B
2.	B	7.	A
3.	C	8.	A
4.	D	9.	D
5.	A	10.	A

TEST 2

DIRECTIONS: Each question consists of a sentence which may or may not be an example of good English usage. Examine each sentence, considering grammar, punctuation, spelling, capitalization, and awkwardness. Then choose the correct statement about it from the four choices below it. If the English usage in the sentence given is better than any of the changes suggested in choices B, C, or D, pick choice A. (Do not pick a choice that will change the meaning of the sentence.) *PRINT THE LETTER OF THE CORRECT ANSWER IN THE SPACE AT THE RIGHT.*

1. The supervisor wants that all staff members report to the office at 9:00 A.M. 1.____
   A. This is an example of acceptable writing.
   B. The word "that" should be removed and the word "to" should be inserted after the word "members."
   C. There should be a comma after the word "wants" and a comma after the word "office."
   D. The word "wants" should be changed to "want" and the word "shall" should be inserted after the word "members."

2. Every morning the clerk opens the office mail and distributes it. 2.____
   A. This is an example of acceptable writing.
   B. The word "opens" should be changed to "open."
   C. The word "mail" should be changed to "letters."
   D. The word "it" should be changed to "them."

3. The secretary typed more fast on a desktop computer than on a laptop computer. 3.____
   A. This is an example of acceptable writing.
   B. The words "more fast" should be changed to "faster."
   C. There should be a comma after the words "desktop computer."
   D. The word "than" should be changed to "then."

4. The new stenographer needed a desk a computer, a chair and a blotter. 4.____
   A. This is an example of acceptable writing.
   B. The word "blotter" should be spelled "blodder."
   C. The word "stenographer" should begin with a capital letter.
   D. There should be a comma after the word "desk."

5. The recruiting officer said, "There are many different goverment jobs available." 5.____
   A. This is an example of acceptable writing.
   B. The word "There" should not be capitalized.
   C. The word "government" should be spelled "government."
   D. The comma after the word "said" should be removed.

6. He can recommend a mechanic whose work is reliable. 6.____
   A. This is an example of acceptable writing.
   B. The word "reliable" should be spelled "relyable."
   C. The word "whose" should be spelled "who's."
   D. The word "mechanic should be spelled "mecanic."

7. She typed quickly; like someone who had not a moment to lose. 7.____
   A. This is an example of acceptable writing.
   B. The word "not" should be removed.
   C. The semicolon should be changed to a comma.
   D. The word "quickly" should be placed before instead of after the word "typed."

8. She insisted that she had to much work to do. 8.____
   A. This is an example of acceptable writing.
   B. The word "insisted" should be spelled "incisted."
   C. The word "to" used in front of "much" should be spelled "too."
   D. The word "do" should be changed to "be done."

9. He excepted praise from his supervisor for a job well done. 9.____
   A. This is an example of acceptable writing.
   B. The word "excepted" should be spelled "accepted."
   C. The order of the words "well done" should be changed to "done well."
   D. There should be a comma after the word "supervisor."

10. What appears to be intentional errors in grammar occur several times in the passage. 10.____
    A. This is an example of acceptable writing.
    B. The word "occur" should be spelled "occurr."
    C. The word "appears" should be changed to "appear."
    D. The phrase "several times" should be changed to "from time to time."

KEY (CORRECT ANSWERS)

1.	B	6.	A
2.	A	7.	C
3.	B	8.	C
4.	D	9.	B
5.	C	10.	C

TEST 3

DIRECTIONS: Each question consists of a sentence which may or may not be an example of good English usage. Examine each sentence, considering grammar, punctuation, spelling, capitalization, and awkwardness. Then choose the correct statement about it from the four choices below it. If the English usage in the sentence given is better than any of the changes suggested in choices B, C, or D, pick choice A. (Do not pick a choice that will change the meaning of the sentence.) *PRINT THE LETTER OF THE CORRECT ANSWER IN THE SPACE AT THE RIGHT.*

1. The clerk could have completed the assignment on time if he knows where these materials were located.
   A. This is an example of acceptable writing.
   B. The word "knows" should be replaced by "had known."
   C. The word "were" should be replaced by "had been."
   D. The words "where these materials were located" should be replaced by "the location of these materials."

2. All employees should be given safety training. Not just those who accidents.
   A. This is an example of acceptable writing.
   B. The period after the word "training" should be changed to a colon.
   C. The period after the word "training" should be changed to a semicolon, and the first letter of the word "Not" should be changed to a small "n."
   D. The period after the word "training" should be changed to a comma, and the first letter of the word "Not" should be changed to a small "n."

3. This proposal is designed to promote employee awareness of the suggestion program, to encourage employee participation in the program, and to increase the number of suggestions submitted.
   A. This is an example of acceptable writing.
   B. The word "proposal" should be spelled "proposal."
   C. The words "to increase the number of suggestions submitted" should be changed to "an increase in the number of suggestions is expected."
   D. The word "promote" should be changed to "enhance" and the word "increase" should be changed to "add to."

4. The introduction of inovative managerial techniques should be preceded by careful analysis of the specific circumstances and conditions in each department.
   A. This is an example of acceptable writing.
   B. The word "technique" should be spelled "techneques."
   C. The word "inovative" should be spelled "innovative."
   D. A comma should be placed after the word "circumstances" and after the word "conditions."

129

5. This occurrence indicates that such criticism embarrasses him.
   A. This is an example of acceptable writing.
   B. The word "occurrence" should be spelled "occurence."
   C. The word "criticism" should be spelled "critisism."
   D. The word "embarrasses" should be spelled "embarasses."

KEY (CORRECT ANSWERS)

1. B
2. D
3. A
4. C
5. A

PHILOSOPHY, PRINCIPLES, PRACTICES, AND TECHNICS OF SUPERVISION, ADMINISTRATION, MANAGEMENT, AND ORGANIZATION

TABLE OF CONTENTS

	Page
MEANING OF SUPERVISION	1
THE OLD AND THE NEW SUPERVISION	1
THE EIGHT (8) BASIC PRINCIPLES OF THE NEW SUPERVISION	1
I. Principle of Responsibility	1
II. Principle of Authority	2
III. Principle of Self-Growth	2
IV. Principle of Individual Worth	2
V. Principle of Creative Leadership	2
VI. Principle of Success and Failure	2
VII. Principle of Science	3
VIII. Principle of Cooperation	3
WHAT IS ADMINISTRATION?	3
I. Practices Commonly Classed as "Supervisory"	3
II. Practices Commonly Classed as "Administrative"	3
III. Practices Commonly Classed as Both "Supervisory" and "Administrative"	4
RESPONSIBILITIES OF THE SUPERVISOR	4
COMPETENCIES OF THE SUPERVISOR	4
THE PROFESSIONAL SUPERVISOR-EMPLOYEE RELATIONSHIP	4
MINI-TEXT IN SUPERVISION, ADMINISTRATION, MANAGEMENT, AND ORGANIZATION	5
I. Brief Highlights	5
A. Levels of Management	6
B. What the Supervisor Must Learn	6
C. A Definition of Supervision	6
D. Elements of the Team Concept	6
E. Principles of Organization	6
F. The Four Important Parts of Every Job	7
G. Principles of Delegation	7
H. Principles of Effective Communications	7
I. Principles of Work Improvement	7
J. Areas of Job Improvement	7
K. Seven Key Points in Making Improvements	8

	L.	Corrective Techniques for Job Improvement	8
	M.	A Planning Checklist	8
	N.	Five Characteristics of Good Directions	9
	O.	Types of Directions	9
	P.	Controls	9
	Q.	Orienting the New Employee	9
	R.	Checklist for Orienting New Employees	9
	S.	Principles of Learning	10
	T.	Causes of Poor Performance	10
	U.	Four Major Steps in On-the-Job Instructions	10
	V.	Employees Want Five Things	10
	W.	Some Don'ts in Regard to Praise	11
	X.	How to Gain Your Workers' Confidence	11
	Y.	Sources of Employee Problems	11
	Z.	The Supervisor's Key to Discipline	11
	AA.	Five Important Processes of Management	12
	BB.	When the Supervisor Fails to Plan	12
	CC.	Fourteen General Principles of Management	12
	DD.	Change	12
II.	Brief Topical Summaries		13
	A.	Who/What is the Supervisor?	13
	B.	The Sociology of Work	13
	C.	Principles and Practices of Supervision	14
	D.	Dynamic Leadership	14
	E.	Processes for Solving Problems	15
	F.	Training for Results	15
	G.	Health, Safety, and Accident Prevention	16
	H.	Equal Employment Opportunity	16
	I.	Improving Communications	16
	J.	Self-Development	17
	K.	Teaching and Training	17
		1. The Teaching Process	17
		a. Preparation	17
		b. Presentation	18
		c. Summary	18
		d. Application	18
		e. Evaluation	18
		2. Teaching Methods	18
		a. Lecture	18
		b. Discussion	18
		c. Demonstration	19
		d. Performance	19
		e. Which Method to Use	19

PHILOSOPHY, PRINCIPLES, PRACTICES, AND TECHNICS OF SUPERVISION, ADMINISTRATION, MANAGEMENT, AND ORGANIZATION

MEANING OF SUPERVISION

The extension of the democratic philosophy has been accompanied by an extension in the scope of supervision. Modern leaders and supervisors no longer think of supervision in the narrow sense of being confined chiefly to visiting employees, supplying materials, or rating the staff. They regard supervision as being intimately related to all the concerned agencies of society, they speak of the supervisor's function in terms of "growth," rather than the "improvement" of employees.

This modern concept of supervision may be defined as follows: Supervision is leadership and the development of leadership within groups which are cooperatively engaged in inspection, research, training, guidance, and evaluation.

THE OLD AND THE NEW SUPERVISION

TRADITIONAL
1. Inspection
2. Focused on the employee
3. Visitation
4. Random and haphazard
5. Imposed and authoritarian
6. One person usually

MODERN
1. Study and analysis
2. Focused on aims, materials, methods, supervisors, employees, environment
3. Demonstrations, intervisitation, workshops, directed reading, bulletins, etc.
4. Definitely organized and planned (scientific)
5. Cooperative and democratic
6. Many persons involved (creative)

THE EIGHT (8) BASIC PRINCIPLES OF THE NEW SUPERVISION

I. Principle of Responsibility
    Authority to act and responsibility for acting must be joined.
    A. If you give responsibility, give authority.
    B. Define employee duties clearly.
    C. Protect employees from criticism by others.
    D. Recognize the rights as well as obligations of employees.
    E. Achieve the aims of a democratic society insofar as it is possible within the area of your work.
    F. Establish a situation favorable to training and learning.
    G. Accept ultimate responsibility for everything done in your section, unit, office, division, department.
    H. Good administration and good supervision are inseparable.

II. Principle of Authority
The success of the supervisor is measured by the extent to which the power of authority is not used.
   A. Exercise simplicity and informality in supervision
   B. Use the simplest machinery of supervision
   C. If it is good for the organization as a whole, it is probably justified.
   D. Seldom be arbitrary or authoritative.
   E. Do not base your work on the power of position or of personality.
   F. Permit and encourage the free expression of opinions.

III. Principle of Self-Growth
The success of the supervisor is measured by the extent to which, and the speed with which, he is no longer needed.
   A. Base criticism on principles, not on specifics.
   B. Point out higher activities to employees.
   C. Train for self-thinking by employees to meet new situations.
   D. Stimulate initiative, self-reliance, and individual responsibility
   E. Concentrate on stimulating the growth of employees rather than on removing defects.

IV. Principle of Individual Worth
Respect for the individual is a paramount consideration in supervision.
   A. Be human and sympathetic in dealing with employees.
   B. Don't nag about things to be done.
   C. Recognize the individual differences among employees and seek opportunities to permit best expression of each personality.

V. Principle of Creative Leadership
The best supervision is that which is not apparent to the employee.
   A. Stimulate, don't drive employees to creative action.
   B. Emphasize doing good things.
   C. Encourage employees to do what they do best.
   D. Do not be too greatly concerned with details of subject or method.
   E. Do not be concerned exclusively with immediate problems and activities.
   F. Reveal higher activities and make them both desired and maximally possible.
   G. Determine procedures in the light of each situation but see that these are derived from a sound basic philosophy.
   H. Aid, inspire, and lead so as to liberate the creative spirit latent in all good employees.

VI. Principle of Success and Failure
There are no unsuccessful employees, only unsuccessful supervisors who have failed to give proper leadership.
   A. Adapt suggestions to the capacities, attitudes, and prejudices of employees.
   B. Be gradual, be progressive, be persistent.
   C. Help the employee find the general principle; have the employee apply his own problem to the general principle.
   D. Give adequate appreciation for good work and honest effort.
   E. Anticipate employee difficulties and help to prevent them.
   F. Encourage employees to do the desirable things they will do anyway.
   G. Judge your supervision by the results it secures.

VII. Principle of Science
Successful supervision is scientific, objective, and experimental. It is based on facts, not on prejudices.
   A. Be cumulative in results.
   B. Never divorce your suggestions from the goals of training.
   C. Don't be impatient of results.
   D. Keep all matters on a professional, not a personal, level.
   E. Do not be concerned exclusively with immediate problems and activities.
   F. Use objective means of determining achievement and rating where possible.

VIII. Principle of Cooperation
Supervision is a cooperative enterprise between supervisor and employee.
   A. Begin with conditions as they are.
   B. Ask opinions of all involved when formulating policies.
   C. Organization is as good as its weakest link.
   D. Let employees help to determine policies and department programs.
   E. Be approachable and accessible—physically and mentally.
   F. Develop pleasant social relationships.

WHAT IS ADMINISTRATION

Administration is concerned with providing the environment, the material facilities, and the operational procedures that will promote the maximum growth and development of supervisors and employees. (Organization is an aspect and a concomitant of administration.)

There is no sharp line of demarcation between supervision and administration; these functions are intimately interrelated and, often, overlapping. They are complementary activities.

I. Practices Commonly Classed as "Supervisory"
   A. Conducting employees' conferences
   B. Visiting sections, units, offices, divisions, departments
   C. Arranging for demonstrations
   D. Examining plans
   E. Suggesting professional reading
   F. Interpreting bulletins
   G. Recommending in-service training courses
   H. Encouraging experimentation
   I. Appraising employee morale
   J. Providing for intervisitation

II. Practices Commonly Classified as "Administrative"
   A. Management of the office
   B. Arrangement of schedules for extra duties
   C. Assignment of rooms or areas
   D. Distribution of supplies
   E. Keeping records and reports
   F. Care of audio-visual materials
   G. Keeping inventory records
   H. Checking record cards and books

    I.   Programming special activities
    J.   Checking on the attendance and punctuality of employees

III. Practices Commonly Classified as Both "Supervisory" and "Administrative"
    A.   Program construction
    B.   Testing or evaluating outcomes
    C.   Personnel accounting
    D.   Ordering instructional materials

RESPONSIBILITIES OF THE SUPERVISOR

A person employed in a supervisory capacity must constantly be able to improve his own efficiency and ability. He represent the employer to the employees and only continuous self-examination can make him a capable supervisor.

Leadership and training are the supervisor's responsibility. An efficient working unit is one in which the employees work with the supervisor. It is his job to bring out the best in his employees. He must always be relaxed, courteous, and calm in his association with his employees. Their feelings are important, and a harsh attitude does not develop the most efficient employees.

COMPETENCES OF THE SUPERVISOR

    I.   Complete knowledge of the duties and responsibilities of his position.
    II.   To be able to organize a job, plan ahead, and carry through.
    III. To have self-confidence and initiative.
    IV.   To be able to handle the unexpected situation and make quick decisions.
    V.   To be able to properly train subordinates in the positions they are best suited for.
    VI.   To be able to keep good human relations among his subordinates.
    VII. To be able to keep good human relations between his subordinates and himself and to earn their respect and trust.

THE PROFESSIONAL SUPERVISOR-EMPLOYEE RELATIONSHIP

There are two kinds of efficiency: one kind is only apparent and is produced in organizations through the exercise of mere discipline; this is but a simulation of the second, or true, efficiency which springs from spontaneous cooperation. If you are a manager, no matter how great or small your responsibility, it is your job, in the final analysis, to create and develop this involuntary cooperation among the people whom you supervise. For, no matter how powerful a combination of money, machines, and materials a company may have, this is a dead and sterile thing without a team of willing, thinking, and articulate people to guide it.

The following 21 points are presented as indicative of the exemplary basic relationship that should exist between supervisor and employee:

1. Each person wants to be liked and respected by his fellow employee and wants to be treated with consideration and respect by his superior.
2. The most competent employee will make an error. However, in a unit where good relations exist between the supervisor and his employees, tenseness and fear do not exist. Thus, errors are not hidden or covered up, and the efficiency of a unit is not impaired.

3. Subordinates resent rules, regulations, or orders that are unreasonable or unexplained.
4. Subordinates are quick to resent unfairness, harshness, injustices, and favoritism.
5. An employee will accept responsibility if he knows that he will be complimented for a job well done, and not too harshly chastised for failure; that his supervisor will check the cause of the failure, and, if it was the supervisor's fault, he will assume the blame therefore. If it was the employee's fault, his supervisor will explain the correct method or means of handling the responsibility.
6. An employee wants to receive credit for a suggestion he has made, that is used. If a suggestion cannot be used, the employee is entitled to an explanation. The supervisor should not say "no" and close the subject.
7. Fear and worry slow up a worker's ability. Poor working environment can impair his physical and mental health. A good supervisor avoids forceful methods, threats, and arguments to get a job done.
8. A forceful supervisor is able to train his employees individually and as a team, and is able to motivate them in the proper channels.
9. A mature supervisor is able to properly evaluate his subordinates and to keep them happy and satisfied.
10. A sensitive supervisor will never patronize his subordinates.
11. A worthy supervisor will respect his employees' confidences.
12. Definite and clear-cut responsibilities should be assigned to each executive.
13. Responsibility should always be coupled with corresponding authority.
14. No change should be made in the scope or responsibilities of a position without a definite understanding to that effect on the part of all persons concerned.
15. No executive or employee, occupying a single position in the organization, should be subject to definite orders from more than one source.
16. Orders should never be given to subordinates over the head of a responsible executive. Rather than do this, the officer in question should be supplanted.
17. Criticisms of subordinates should, whoever possible, be made privately, and in no case should a subordinate be criticized in the presence of executives or employees of equal or lower rank.
18. No dispute or difference between executives or employees as to authority or responsibilities should be considered too trivial for prompt and careful adjudication.
19. Promotions, wage changes, and disciplinary action should always be approved by the executive immediately superior to the one directly responsible.
20. No executive or employee should ever be required, or expected, to be at the same time an assistant to, and critic of, another.
21. Any executive whose work is subject to regular inspection should, wherever practicable, be given the assistance and facilities necessary to enable him to maintain an independent check of the quality of his work.

MINI-TEXT IN SUPERVISION, ADMINISTRATION, MANAGEMENT, AND ORGANIZATION

I. Brief Highlights

Listed concisely and sequentially are major headings and important data in the field for quick recall and review.

A. Levels of Management
Any organization of some size has several levels of management. In terms of a ladder, the levels are:

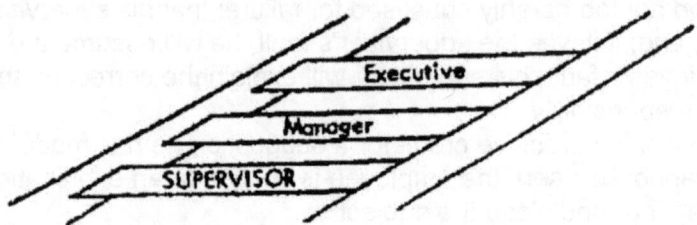

The first level is very important because it is the beginning point of management leadership.

B. What the Supervisor Must Learn
A supervisor must learn to:
1. Deal with people and their differences
2. Get the job done through people
3. Recognize the problems when they exist
4. Overcome obstacles to good performance
5. Evaluate the performance of people
6. Check his own performance in terms of accomplishment

C. A Definition of Supervisor
The term supervisor means any individual having authority, in the interests of the employer, to hire, transfer, suspend, lay-off, recall, promote, discharge, assign, reward, or discipline other employees or responsibility to direct them, or to adjust their grievances, or effectively to recommend such action, if, in connection with the foregoing, exercise of such authority is not of a merely routine or clerical nature but requires the use of independent judgment.

D. Elements of the Team Concept
What is involved in teamwork? The component parts are:
1. Members
2. A leader
3. Goals
4. Plans
5. Cooperation
6. Spirit

E. Principles of Organization
1. A team member must know what his job is.
2. Be sure that the nature and scope of a job are understood.
3. Authority and responsibility should be carefully spelled out.
4. A supervisor should be permitted to make the maximum number of decisions affecting his employees.
5. Employees should report to only one supervisor.
6. A supervisor should direct only as many employees as he can handle effectively.
7. An organization plan should be flexible.

8. Inspection and performance of work should be separate.
9. Organizational problems should receive immediate attention.
10. Assign work in line with ability and experience.

F. The Four Important Parts of Every Job
1. Inherent in every job is the *accountability* for results.
2. A second set of factors in every job is *responsibilities*.
3. Along with duties and responsibilities one must have the *authority* to act within certain limits without obtaining permission to proceed.
4. No job exists in a vacuum. The supervisor is surrounded by key *relationships*.

G. Principles of Delegation
Where work is delegated for the first time, the supervisor should think in terms of these questions:
1. Who is best qualified to do this?
2. Can an employee improve his abilities by doing this?
3. How long should an employee spend on this?
4. Are there any special problems for which he will need guidance?
5. How broad a delegation can I make?

H. Principles of Effective Communications
1. Determine the media.
2. To whom directed?
3. Identification and source authority.
4. Is communication understood?

I. Principles of Work Improvement
1. Most people usually do only the work which is assigned to them.
2. Workers are likely to fit assigned work into the time available to perform it.
3. A good workload usually stimulates output.
4. People usually do their best work when they know that results will be reviewed or inspected.
5. Employees usually feel that someone else is responsible for conditions of work, workplace layout, job methods, type of tools/equipment, and other such factors.
6. Employees are usually defensive about their job security.
7. Employees have natural resistance to change.
8. Employees can support or destroy a supervisor.
9. A supervisor usually earns the respect of his people through his personal example of diligence and efficiency.

J. Areas of Job Improvement
The areas of job improvement are quite numerous, but the most common ones which a supervisor can identify and utilize are:
1. Departmental layout
2. Flow of work
3. Workplace layout
4. Utilization of manpower
5. Work methods
6. Materials handling

7. Utilization
8. Motion economy

K. Seven Key Points in Making Improvements
1. Select the job to be improved
2. Study how it is being done now
3. Question the present method
4. Determine actions to be taken
5. Chart proposed method
6. Get approval and apply
7. Solicit worker participation

L. Corrective Techniques of Job Improvement
Specific Problems
1. Size of workload
2. Inability to meet schedules
3. Strain and fatigue
4. Improper use of men and skills
5. Waste, poor quality, unsafe conditions
6. Bottleneck conditions that hinder output
7. Poor utilization of equipment and machine
8. Efficiency and productivity of labor

General Improvement
1. Departmental layout
2. Flow of work
3. Work plan layout
4. Utilization of manpower
5. Work methods
6. Materials handling
7. Utilization of equipment
8. Motion economy

Corrective Techniques
1. Study with scale model
2. Flow chart study
3. Motion analysis
4. Comparison of units produced to standard allowance
5. Methods analysis
6. Flow chart and equipment study
7. Down time vs. running time
8. Motion analysis

M. A Planning Checklist
1. Objectives
2. Controls
3. Delegations
4. Communications
5. Resources
6. Manpower

7. Equipment
8. Supplies and materials
9. Utilization of time
10. Safety
11. Money
12. Work
13. Timing of improvements

N. Five Characteristics of Good Directions
In order to get results, directions must be:
1. Possible of accomplishment
2. Agreeable with worker interests
3. Related to mission
4. Planned and complete
5. Unmistakably clear

O. Types of Directions
1. Demands or direct orders
2. Requests
3. Suggestion or implication
4. volunteering

P. Controls
A typical listing of the overall areas in which the supervisor should establish controls might be:
1. Manpower
2. Materials
3. Quality of work
4. Quantity of work
5. Time
6. Space
7. Money
8. Methods

Q. Orienting the New Employee
1. Prepare for him
2. Welcome the new employee
3. Orientation for the job
4. Follow-up

R. Checklist for Orienting New Employees   Yes   No
1. Do you appreciate the feelings of new employees
   when they first report for work?   ___   ___
2. Are you aware of the fact that the new employee must
   make a big adjustment to his job?   ___   ___
3. Have you given him good reasons for liking the job and
   the organization?   ___   ___
4. Have you prepared for his first day on the job?   ___   ___
5. Did you welcome him cordially and make him feel needed?   ___   ___

	Yes	No

6. Did you establish rapport with him so that he feels free to talk and discuss matters with you? ___ ___
7. Did you explain his job to him and his relationship to you? ___ ___
8. Does he know that his work will be evaluated periodically on a basis that is fair and objective? ___ ___
9. Did you introduce him to his fellow workers in such a way that they are likely to accept him? ___ ___
10. Does he know what employee benefits he will receive? ___ ___
11. Does he understand the importance of being on the job and what to do if he must leave his duty station? ___ ___
12. Has he been impressed with the importance of accident prevention and safe practice? ___ ___
13. Does he generally know his way around the department? ___ ___
14. Is he under the guidance of a sponsor who will teach the right way of doing things? ___ ___
15. Do you plan to follow-up so that he will continue to adjust successfully to his job? ___ ___

S. Principles of Learning
1. Motivation
2. Demonstration or explanation
3. Practice

T. Causes of Poor Performance
1. Improper training for job
2. Wrong tools
3. Inadequate directions
4. Lack of supervisory follow-up
5. Poor communications
6. Lack of standards of performance
7. Wrong work habits
8. Low morale
9. Other

U. Four Major Steps in On-The-Job Instruction
1. Prepare the worker
2. Present the operation
3. Tryout performance
4. Follow-up

V. Employees Want Five Things
1. Security
2. Opportunity
3. Recognition
4. Inclusion
5. Expression

W. Some Don'ts in Regard to Praise
   1. Don't praise a person for something he hasn't done.
   2. Don't praise a person unless you can be sincere.
   3. Don't be sparing in praise just because your superior withholds it from you.
   4. Don't let too much time elapse between good performance and recognition of it

X. How to Gain Your Workers' Confidence
   Methods of developing confidence include such things as:
   1. Knowing the interests, habits, hobbies of employees
   2. Admitting your own inadequacies
   3. Sharing and telling of confidence in others
   4. Supporting people when they are in trouble
   5. Delegating matters that can be well handled
   6. Being frank and straightforward about problems and working conditions
   7. Encouraging others to bring their problems to you
   8. Taking action on problems which impede worker progress

Y. Sources of Employee Problems
   On-the-job causes might be such things as:
   1. A feeling that favoritism is exercised in assignments
   2. Assignment of overtime
   3. An undue amount of supervision
   4. Changing methods or systems
   5. Stealing of ideas or trade secrets
   6. Lack of interest in job
   7. Threat of reduction in force
   8. Ignorance or lack of communications
   9. Poor equipment
   10. Lack of knowing how supervisor feels toward employee
   11. Shift assignments

   Off-the-job problems might have to do with:
   1. Health
   2. Finances
   3. Housing
   4. Family

Z. The Supervisor's Key to Discipline
   There are several key points about discipline which the supervisor should keep in mind:
   1. Job discipline is one of the disciplines of life and is directed by the supervisor.
   2. It is more important to correct an employee fault than to fix blame for it.
   3. Employee performance is affected by problems both on the job and off.
   4. Sudden or abrupt changes in behavior can be indications of important employee problems.
   5. Problems should be dealt with as soon as possible after they are identified.
   6. The attitude of the supervisor may have more to do with solving problems than the techniques of problem solving.
   7. Correction of employee behavior should be resorted to only after the supervisor is sure that training or counseling will not be helpful.

8. Be sure to document your disciplinary actions.
9. Make sure that you are disciplining on the basis of facts rather than personal feelings.
10. Take each disciplinary step in order, being careful not to make snap judgments, or decisions based on impatience.

AA. Five Important Processes of Management
1. Planning
2. Organizing
3. Scheduling
4. Controlling
5. Motivating

BB. When the Supervisor Fails to Plan
1. Supervisor creates impression of not knowing his job
2. May lead to excessive overtime
3. Job runs itself—supervisor lacks control
4. Deadlines and appointments missed
5. Parts of the work go undone
6. Work interrupted by emergencies
7. Sets a bad example
8. Uneven workload creates peaks and valleys
9. Too much time on minor details at expense of more important tasks

CC. Fourteen General Principles of Management
1. Division of work
2. Authority and responsibility
3. Discipline
4. Unity of command
5. Unity of direction
6. Subordination of individual interest to general interest
7. Remuneration of personnel
8. Centralization
9. Scalar chain
10. Order
11. Equity
12. Stability of tenure of personnel
13. Initiative
14. Esprit de corps

DD. Change

Bringing about change is perhaps attempted more often, and yet less well understood, than anything else the supervisor does. How do people generally react to change? (People tend to resist change that is imposed upon them by other individuals or circumstances.

Change is characteristic of every situation. It is a part of every real endeavor where the efforts of people are concerned.

1. Why do people resist change?
   People may resist change because of:
   a. Fear of the unknown
   b. Implied criticism
   c. Unpleasant experiences in the past
   d. Fear of loss of status
   e. Threat to the ego
   f. Fear of loss of economic stability

2. How can we best overcome the resistance to change?
   In initiating change, take these steps:
   a. Get ready to sell
   b. Identify sources of help
   c. Anticipate objections
   d. Sell benefits
   e. Listen in depth
   f. Follow up

II. Brief Topical Summaries

   A. Who/What is the Supervisor?
      1. The supervisor is often called the "highest level employee and the lowest level manager."
      2. A supervisor is a member of both management and the work group. He acts as a bridge between the two.
      3. Most problems in supervision are in the area of human relations, or people problems.
      4. Employees expect: Respect, opportunity to learn and to advance, and a sense of belonging, and so forth.
      5. Supervisors are responsible for directing people and organizing work. Planning is of paramount importance.
      6. A position description is a set of duties and responsibilities inherent to a given position.
      7. It is important to keep the position description up-to-date and to provide each employee with his own copy.

   B. The Sociology of Work
      1. People are alike in many ways; however, each individual is unique.
      2. The supervisor is challenged in getting to know employee differences. Acquiring skills in evaluating individuals is an asset.
      3. Maintaining meaningful working relationships in the organization is of great importance.
      4. The supervisor has an obligation to help individuals to develop to their fullest potential.
      5. Job rotation on a planned basis helps to build versatility and to maintain interest and enthusiasm in work groups.
      6. Cross training (job rotation) provides backup skills.

7. The supervisor can help reduce tension by maintaining a sense of humor, providing guidance to employees, and by making reasonable and timely decisions. Employees respond favorably to working under reasonably predictable circumstances.
8. Change is characteristic of all managerial behavior. The supervisor must adjust to changes in procedures, new methods, technological changes, and to a number of new and sometimes challenging situations.
9. To overcome the natural tendency for people to resist change, the supervisor should become more skillful in initiating change.

C. Principles and Practices of Supervision
1. Employees should be required to answer to only one superior.
2. A supervisor can effectively direct only a limited number of employees, depending upon the complexity, variety, and proximity of the jobs involved.
3. The organizational chart presents the organization in graphic form. It reflects lines of authority and responsibility as well as interrelationships of units within the organization.
4. Distribution of work can be improved through an analysis using the "Work Distribution Chart."
5. The "Work Distribution Chart" reflects the division of work within a unit in understandable form.
6. When related tasks are given to an employee, he has a better chance of increasing his skills through training.
7. The individual who is given the responsibility for tasks must also be given the appropriate authority to insure adequate results.
8. The supervisor should delegate repetitive, routine work. Preparation of recurring reports, maintaining leave and attendance records are some examples.
9. Good discipline is essential to good task performance. Discipline is reflected in the actions of employees on the job in the absence of supervision.
10. Disciplinary action may have to be taken when the positive aspects of discipline have failed. Reprimand, warning, and suspension are examples of disciplinary action.
11. If a situation calls for a reprimand, be sure it is deserved and remember it is to be done in private.

D. Dynamic Leadership
1. A style is a personal method or manner of exerting influence.
2. Authoritarian leaders often see themselves as the source of power and authority.
3. The democratic leader often perceives the group as the source of authority and power.
4. Supervisors tend to do better when using the pattern of leadership that is most natural for them.
5. Social scientists suggest that the effective supervisor use the leadership style that best fits the problem or circumstances involved.
6. All four styles—telling, selling, consulting, joining—have their place. Using one does not preclude using the other at another time.

7. The theory X point of view assumes that the average person dislikes work, will avoid it whenever possible, and must be coerced to achieve organizational objectives.
8. The theory Y point of view assumes that the average person considers work to be a natural as play, and, when the individual is committed, he requires little supervision or direction to accomplish desired objectives.
9. The leader's basic assumptions concerning human behavior and human nature affect his actions, decisions, and other managerial practices.
10. Dissatisfaction among employees is often present, but difficult to isolate. The supervisor should seek to weaken dissatisfaction by keeping promises, being sincere and considerate, keeping employees informed, and so forth.
11. Constructive suggestions should be encouraged during the natural progress of the work.

E. Processes for Solving Problems
1. People find their daily tasks more meaningful and satisfying when they can improve them.
2. The causes of problems, or the key factors, are often hidden in the background. Ability to solve problems often involves the ability to isolate them from their backgrounds. There is some substance to the cliché that some persons "can't see the forest for the trees."
3. New procedures are often developed from old ones. Problems should be broken down into manageable parts. New ideas can be adapted from old one.
4. People think differently in problem-solving situations. Using a logical, patterned approach is often useful. One approach found to be useful includes these steps:
   a. Define the problem
   b. Establish objectives
   c. Get the facts
   d. Weigh and decide
   e. Take action
   f. Evaluate action

F. Training for Results
1. Participants respond best when they feel training is important to them.
2. The supervisor has responsibility for the training and development of those who report to him.
3. When training is delegated to others, great care must be exercised to insure the trainer has knowledge, aptitude, and interest for his work as a trainer.
4. Training (learning) of some type goes on continually. The most successful supervisor makes certain the learning contributes in a productive manner to operational goals.
5. New employees are particularly susceptible to training. Older employees facing new job situations require specific training, as well as having need for development and growth opportunities.
6. Training needs require continuous monitoring.
7. The training officer of an agency is a professional with a responsibility to assist supervisors in solving training problems.

8. Many of the self-development steps important to the supervisor's own growth are equally important to the development of peers and subordinates. Knowledge of these is important when the supervisor consults with others on development and growth opportunities.

G. Health, Safety, and Accident Prevention
1. Management-minded supervisors take appropriate measures to assist employees in maintaining health and in assuring safe practices in the work environment.
2. Effective safety training and practices help to avoid injury and accidents.
3. Safety should be a management goal. All infractions of safety which are observed should be corrected without exception.
4. Employees' safety attitude, training and instruction, provision of safe tools and equipment, supervision, and leadership are considered highly important factors which contribute to safety and which can be influenced directly by supervisors.
5. When accidents do occur, they should be investigated promptly for very important reasons, including the fact that information which is gained can be used to prevent accidents in the future.

H. Equal Employment Opportunity
1. The supervisor should endeavor to treat all employees fairly, without regard to religion, race, sex, or national origin.
2. Groups tend to reflect the attitude of the leader. Prejudice can be detected even in very subtle form. Supervisors must strive to create a feeling of mutual respect and confidence in every employee.
3. Complete utilization of all human resources is a national goal. Equitable consideration should be accorded women in the work force, minority-group members, the physically and mentally handicapped, and the older employee. The important question is: "Who can do the job?"
4. Training opportunities, recognition for performance, overtime assignments, promotional opportunities, and all other personnel actions are to be handled on an equitable basis.

I. Improving Communications
1. Communications is achieving understanding between the sender and the receiver of a message. It also means sharing information—the creation of understanding.
2. Communication is basic to all human activity. Words are means of conveying meanings; however, real meanings are in people.
3. There are very practical differences in the effectiveness of one-way, impersonal, and two-way communications. Words spoken face-to-face are better understood. Telephone conversations are effective, but lack the rapport of person-to-person exchanges. The whole person communicates.
4. Cooperation and communication in an organization go hand in hand. When there is a mutual respect between people, spelling out rules and procedures for communicating is unnecessary.
5. There are several barriers to effective communications. These include failure to listen with respect and understanding, lack of skill in feedback, and misinterpreting the meanings of words used by the speaker. It is also common

practice to listen to what we want to hear, and tune out things we do not want to hear.
6. Communication is management's chief problem. The supervisor should accept the challenge to communicate more effectively and to improve interagency and intra-agency communications.
7. The supervisor may often plan for and conduct meetings. The planning phase is critical and may determine the success or the failure of a meeting.
8. Speaking before groups usually requires extra effort. Stage fright may never disappear completely, but it can be controlled.

J. Self-Development
1. Every employee is responsible for his own self-development.
2. Toastmaster and toastmistress clubs offer opportunities to improve skills in oral communications.
3. Planning for one's own self-development is of vital importance. Supervisors know their own strengths and limitations better than anyone else.
4. Many opportunities are open to aid the supervisor in his developmental efforts, including job assignments; training opportunities, both governmental and non-governmental—to include universities and professional conferences and seminars.
5. Programmed instruction offers a means of studying at one's own rate.
6. Where difficulties may arise from a supervisor's being away from his work for training, he may participate in televised home study or correspondence courses to meet his self-development needs.

K. Teaching and Training
1. The Teaching Process
Teaching is encouraging and guiding the learning activities of students toward established goals. In most cases this process consists of five steps: preparation, presentation, summarization, evaluation, and application.

   a. Preparation
   Preparation is two-fold in nature; that of the supervisor and the employee. Preparation by the supervisor is absolutely essential to success. He must know what, when, where, how, and whom he will teach. Some of the factors that should be considered are:
   1) The objectives
   2) The materials needed
   3) The methods to be used
   4) Employee participation
   5) Employee interest
   6) Training aids
   7) Evaluation
   8) Summarization

   Employee preparation consists in preparing the employee to receive the material. Probably the most important single factor in the preparation of the employee is arousing and maintaining his interest. He must know the objectives of the training, why he is there, how the material can be used, and its importance to him.

b. Presentation
   In presentation, have a carefully designed plan and follow it. The plan should be accurate and complete, yet flexible enough to meet situations as they arise. The method of presentation will be determined by the particular situation and objectives.

c. Summary
   A summary should be made at the end of every training unit and program. In addition, there may be internal summaries depending on the nature of the material being taught. The important thing is that the trainee must always be able to understand how each part of the new material relates to the whole.

d. Application
   The supervisor must arrange work so the employee will be given a chance to apply new knowledge or skills while the material is still clear in his mind and interest is high. The trainee does not really know whether he has learned the material until he has been given a chance to apply it. If the material is not applied, it loses most of its value.

e. Evaluation
   The purpose of all training is to promote learning. To determine whether the training has been a success or failure, the supervisor must evaluate this learning.
   In the broadest sense, evaluation includes all the devices, methods, skills, and techniques used by the supervisor to keep himself and the employees informed as to their progress toward the objectives they are pursuing. The extent to which the employee has mastered the knowledge, skills, and abilities, or changed his attitudes, as determined by the program objectives, is the extent to which instruction has succeeded or failed.
   Evaluation should not be confined to the end of the lesson, day, or program but should be used continuously. We shall note later the way this relates to the rest of the teaching process.

2. Teaching Methods
   A teaching method is a pattern of identifiable student and instructor activity used in presenting training material.
   All supervisors are faced with the problem of deciding which method should be used at a given time.

   a. Lecture
      The lecture is direct oral presentation of material by the supervisor. The present trend is to place less emphasis on the trainer's activity and more on that of the trainee.

   b. Discussion
      Teaching by discussion or conference involves using questions and other techniques to arouse interest and focus attention upon certain areas, and by doing so creating a learning situation. This can be one of the most

valuable methods because it gives the employees an opportunity to express their ideas and pool their knowledge.

c. Demonstration
The demonstration is used to teach how something works or how to do something. It can be used to show a principle or what the results of a series of actions will be. A well-staged demonstration is particularly effective because it shows proper methods of performance in a realistic manner.

d. Performance
Performance is one of the most fundamental of all learning techniques or teaching methods. The trainee may be able to tell how a specific operation should be performed but he cannot be sure he knows how to perform the operation until he has done so.
As with all methods, there are certain advantages and disadvantages to each method.

e. Which Method to Use
Moreover, there are other methods and techniques of teaching. It is difficult to use any method without other methods entering into it. In any learning situation, a combination of methods is usually more effective than any one method alone.

Finally, evaluation must be integrated into the other aspects of the teaching-learning process.

It must be used in the motivation of the trainees; it must be used to assist in developing understanding during the training; and it must be related to employee application of the results of training.

This is distinctly the role of the supervisor.

www.ingramcontent.com/pod-product-compliance
Lightning Source LLC
Chambersburg PA
CBHW081821300426
44116CB00014B/2437